Sara Ann Key is a mother of four grown up children and lives in Royal Tunbridge Wells Kent and is a professional Nanny and armchair psychologist.

Working primarily in the early years of the childcare sector, she specialises in working with neuro diverse children and their families. Passionate about providing children with the best possible start in life, Sara advocates a holistic approach to parenting.

In her spare time, she can be found strolling amongst the beautiful Kent countryside pondering the meaning of life and also, when she can, enjoys travelling to far-flung places.

A protagonist at heart, Sara follows a universal pattern whereby she is undergoing a spiritual transformation that changes the way she sees herself to empower her life.

Dedicated to Marilyn Gibson

Sara Ann Key

THE JOURNEY CONTINUES

AUSTIN MACAULEY PUBLISHERS™

LONDON • CAMBRIDGE • NEW YORK • SHARJAH

A CIP catalogue record for this title is available from the British Library.

ISBN 9781035841035 (Paperback)
ISBN 9781035841042 (ePub e-book)

www.austinmacauley.com

First Published 2024
Austin Macauley Publishers Ltd®
1 Canada Square
Canary Wharf
London
E14 5AA

Gabor Mate
Eckhart Tolle

Preface

Before we get into this book, it is entirely natural for you to want to know why you would want to read about my spiritual journey and transformation, which I feel called to make mainly to awaken a deeper understanding of my sacred contract and higher purpose, and why you should be interested in that. Each of us living within the physical world is a spirit person within a physical body.

Awareness of who we truly are spiritually can be hugely beneficial to a person who searches for this. Acknowledging our own spirit, the eternal part of self has a wonderfully liberating effect on our awareness as there we can see who we really are and what we need to achieve while here on earth.

In order to grow, we have to understand that some things that have happened in our lives were beyond our control. When we look back on the past, we may begin to wonder that if we had made different choices, perhaps things would have turned out differently or maybe if we were in a certain place at a specific time certain things would not have happened the way they did.

Following on from my first book, *The Journey,* I want to show you what happened next as I put into practice all the spiritual lessons I have learnt and the miraculous transformation I have made since then. They say everything happens for a reason and that things unfold the way it is meant to be, but often we find that hard to except.

As the personality trait of the protagonist, I follow a universal pattern in which I am undergoing a transformation that changes the way I see myself, and my psychology, and realising my capacity to empower my life. With 25% of the population falling under this umbrella, we are committed to spiritual growth and evolution, and I hope that showing you how I am creating a better way forward personally and collectively, it will inspire you to do the same.

As I relay my life experiences, especially working in the world of children where it all starts with our family experiences and inherited belief systems, I discover that our emotional system is as much a part of our survival as our immune and nervous system is. I look towards the future with introspection and a positive mindset.

With a lifetime of experience behind me, I am able to explain and explore the psychology behind each interaction and event I encountered to guide the reader into a greater understanding of how our actions and experiences have a knock-on effect on ourselves and humanity. The nature of our soul is shaped by the quality of our thoughts—positive, constructive and virtuous thoughts create a bright and vibrant soul, whereas negative or destructive thinking can create a dark and stained soul.

Our thoughts are not just fleeting mental events but are powerful agents that have a lasting impact on our character and inner world. Therefore, it is crucial to be mindful of our thoughts and actively work to create positive and virtuous thinking patterns.

If you would like to change your life, you must first change the way you think about your life. Thoughts are not just thoughts but are bridges, doors, entrance ways, and foundations. They magnetise and repel. Thoughts are investments and they are decisions. They can energise momentum, or keep you idling within your own little world forever. Thoughts create feelings; feelings create desire; desires create actions, and actions create rewards.

Drawing on scientific research, I explore how the mind works, and show you how we can change the way we perceive things and take responsibility for that. I am exploring a deeper and more profound look at my life and showing you that I now have control over the state of my soul and that we can all work together towards creating a brighter, more vibrant inner world.

In this modern-day world that is so frenetic and non-stop full of busyness, I feel that we are losing connection to our souls and consciousness. I want to show you that if we take time to stop and listen, something good really happens.

As I shift my reality from victim to survivor through the powerful reminder of the importance of mindfulness and self-reflection, I can show you that by paying attention to the quality of our thoughts and actively cultivating positive thinking patterns we find empowerment and learn powerful lessons. My ex-husbands may not thank me for this book as I go deeply into the psychology behind why each of those marriages and relationships failed.

For those of you struggling with your own life journey, through all of this process, I want to show you that I am finally finding inner peace and clarity and loving my life and the person that I have become today because of it. In doing so, I hope that you find the same.

Chapter 1

The Corona Virus pandemic in January 2021 prompted the World Health Organisation to declare a global health emergency amid thousands of new cases of the Corona Virus in China, where it all began in 2019.

By May 2021, England had its fifth wettest May on record, and its wettest since 1967, with 111 mm of rain. At this time, according to Gov.UK, there were 4,421,850 lab confirmed cases of the Corona Virus and 127,539 associated deaths in the UK. With the virus still ragging and the vaccine campaigns just under way, the entertainment and hospitality sector had been hit hard by the two lockdowns that had been inflicted on the UK citizens by our government, sending us all into hibernation and isolation primarily to shield us from catching the virus while protecting our NHS.

With the rest of the world attending to the fallout from the pandemic, Britain had its own challenges to overcome. Boris Johnson, our prime minister, made an announcement on 19 May at a Corona Virus press conference to say that there had been further clusters of the B.1.617.2 variant first observed in India. Believing this variant was significantly more transmissible than the previous one, the future economically for the UK was looking unpredictable.

The scale of the vaccine roll out, which PHE estimated had already saved almost 12,000 lives and prevented over 33,000 people from being hospitalised, the country was in a different position from when it faced a new variant the Christmas before. Still, the virus was prone to mutate and concerns as to whether the vaccine would protect us against the new variants had left us all feeling insecure about the future.

It had now been two years since I had left my marriage and been surviving on my own. My profession at this time was still as a professional nanny to my employer, whose job was in the film industry's red carpet award ceremonies sector. Despite the first lockdown, she had managed to muster some remote work and just about survived financially through this difficult period, but by the time the second lockdown hit, her work had dried up, and therefore, my employer soon found herself without an income.

The COVID-19 pandemic had a substantial impact on the film industry in 2020/ 2021 mirroring its impacts across all the arts sector. Across the world, and to varying degrees, cinemas and movie theatres had been closed, festivals cancelled and film releases moved to future dates or delayed indefinitely. Due to cinemas and movie theatres closing, the global box office had dropped by billions of dollars, streaming had seen a significant increase in popularity and the stock of film exhibitors had also dropped dramatically.

Many blockbusters originally scheduled to be released in mid-March 2020 have been postponed or cancelled around the world.

My employer had worked for 20th Century Fox since leaving school and had worked her way up through the ranks advancing to a senior position. For over 80 years, beginning with its founding in 1935 and ending in 2019 (when it became part of Walt Disney Studios), 20th Century was one of the then 'Big Six' major American film studios. Formally known as 20th Century Fox Film Corporation, it was formed in 1935 from the merger of Fox Film Corporation and 20th Century Pictures as one of the original Big Five among 8 majors of Hollywood's Golden Age.

During her time with them, she had attended to and worked with many A-list celebrities mainly from Los Angeles when they had come over to the UK for the BAFTA award ceremony as well as attending to our own British actors. Herself being one of the nominators of the BAFTA, she had put so much business through London's hospitality sector while attending to all their needs, in particular Claridge's Hotel in Mayfair.

She had taken me and the children there in 2019, soon after I had just started working for her while meeting a colleague from LA for a catch-up lunch. I had stayed there previously many years before in the good old days of the Old Rectory when my husband had booked us a suite over Christmas time when it was our ex's turn to have the children. So I knew the hotel well, and therefore, was surprised to find myself back there at this time under very different circumstances.

Well-known there, the chef had personally come out to say hello and greet my employer. It had been an exciting introduction to the new job for me. Lunch had been a memorable experience consisting of the finest beef fillet steak with truffle-infused potatoes, washed down with a delicious fine wine. Despite being a working lunch, my employer had been relaxed and generous.

Claridge's was a beautiful hotel. There was an exhibition of the famous artist, Damian Hirsts, in the foyer. A collection of his marine art known as 'Treasures from the wreck of the unbelievable' an awe-inspiring exhibition. Thirteen intriguing sculptures from the Titanic-esque exhibition, in which many still retained their original coral encrustations.

I had been fascinated by the mermaid in the centre of the foyer and had naively gone to touch it when the concierge exclaimed, "Madam, please don't touch it, it's worth millions."

Claridge's Hotel in London was the epitome of timeless elegance and one of the best 5-star luxury hotels in the world, with long-standing connections with royalty. Founded in 1812 as Mivart's Hotel in a conventional London terraced house, it grew by expanding into neighbouring houses. In 1854, the founder (the father of biologist St George Jackson Mivart) sold the hotel to a Mr and Mrs Claridge, who owned a smaller hotel next door.

They combined the two operations, and after trading for a time as 'Mivart's at Claridge's', they settled on the current name. The reputation of the hotel was confirmed in 1860 when Empress Eugenie made an extended visit and entertained Queen Victoria at the hotel. The landmark hotel had a spectacular makeover in 2020 and dug 33m beneath Brook Street to create the most glamorous basement extension in the world, and added an art space housing Damian Hirsts' works.

With my employer now without work and facing new challenges, she kept me on for as long as she possibly could by taking advantage of the government's furlough scheme, but eventually, I soon found myself losing my job as a nanny to her children.

With other sectors reeling from the lockdown and tentatively emerging back into the world with cautious optimism, somewhat like bears after awakening from hibernation as they went through a similar period known as walking hibernation where they had to adjust to being awake, I found myself back on the childcare website looking for a new position.

I loved working for my work family. Although a job, I loved them and they loved me. I found them to be like a true family to me, a highly sensitive family with personality traits like my own, also known as sensory processing sensitivity (SPS), or 'Highly sensitive person', HPS for short. A temperamental trait involves 'an increased sensitivity of the nervous system and a deeper cognitive processing of physical, social and emotional stimuli'.

With 15-25% of the population falling under this umbrella, our brains worked differently from others, whereby we processed information and reflected on it more deeply and were acutely aware of subtitles in our environment.

Very emotional, compassionate and generous people, sensitive to criticism, and with a feeling of being different from everyone else. Sometimes overthinking and worrying and being sensitive to external stimuli, is often regarded as a negative trait or weakness. But feeling deeply was a quality to be valued and celebrated, and to be able to easily pick up on what other people are feeling, and finding our inner lives rich and interesting. I had found my tribe and it had not felt like a job but had felt more like coming home.

My time with them had been an incredible journey of personal transformation, self-discovery and adjustment to my new found independent life as a single woman, after having left my marriage of 23 years, where I had been solely dependent on my husband. We survived the pandemic together and supported one another emotionally and physically through it. I had been asked to be godparent to both of their children and had been given love, trust, security, and comfort for the 18 months I had been with them.

I loved being around the glamour and inside stories of the glamorous world of celebrities and film. I had enjoyed being immersed in the creativity that the family had been gifted with. Indeed, by now, I was a new writer with a published book in front of me and the writing had been born, created and encouraged from that environment.

I was now surprisingly a published author, having written an autobiography and self-help book, while still doing a 60-hour working week, not including overtime. I had worked long and hard, had thrived, and been stimulated in that environment, but for now, I found myself looking for work in an uncertain world. It was hard to leave them, but change was inevitable and it was time to move on.

Around this challenging time, my eldest daughter, who had helped me move into my flat after I had left my husband back in October 2018, sent me a text one morning telling me that her husband who had *initially stood* as a guarantee on my flat, wanted to come off. The timing could not have been worse as I had just lost my job. They had bought a new larger house that they had been renovating, gutting and rebuilding the property from its shell.

Despite my asking them if they could wait until I find a new job and my letting agent warning my son-in-law that this would cause his mother-in-law huge problems by which the tenancy would have to be ended and a new one drawn up, putting me in a very vulnerable position, they refused to wait. With old behavioural patterns emerging of selfishness rearing its ugly head, and perceptions not matching the reality of loved ones' feelings and intentions, the relations naturally became strained once more.

I had tried to explain to my daughter that the letting agent required 3 months of pay checks in order to allow me to take on the new rental agreement and that unfortunately, due to Covid and the reduced income that had occurred from the furlough scheme, my salary did not cover the full 30% rental stipulations required. The shocking realisation was that they both did not appear to care or fully acknowledge that my youngest daughter and I could be left homeless.

Finally, after many hours of sleepless nights, my employers who I had just left working for wrote to the letting agent, stating that they would be employing me again and telling a few fibs to this effect, tried to secure my home for me. Finally, we had managed to secure the tenancy on a six-monthly renewal basis, but it was touch and go and I certainly could not have achieved it without their love and support.

I knew that the next chapter of my life story needed to happen away from the security of that job and the lovely family that had loved and helped me. I had to learn to be financially independent and problem-solve on my own without leaning on other people. I had been told by a psychic medium and a couple of healers that my journey and reasons for coming to this planet and my life's mission must continue with experiences and lessons learnt elsewhere to support my calling.

My belief system and the reason for making sense of my life journey and the things that had happened to me thus far derived from the Buddhist teachings of reincarnation and that we have many lives to live until we reach enlightenment and have paid back karma of past lives, so I embraced the change and moved on.

My new job in contrast was working for a plastic surgeon and her 9 month old son. Originally from Malaysia and with her Irish partner, both individuals were success-driven, busy and proactive. A kind lady but, like all humans, complex and unique. I was starting to notice that being in another person's home, in an intimate and personal space, could be an awkward situation. It was an unusual setting for an employer/ employee relationship.

As such, special attention needed to be directed at its uniqueness to keep everyone healthy and happy. Despite my excellent references and in total contrast to my previous family, I was soon to discover security cameras all over the house and an overly concern for safety and security. I knew after a while I would gain their trust but in the meantime, I had to endure scrutiny suspicion and wariness.

I knew from my study of psychology that this was all fear-based and that something must have happened to them in the past to warrant such extreme behaviour. I had spent 30 years as an autodidact studying psychology and classed myself as a psychotherapist. I wasn't allowed out of the house with the baby for weeks, the pandemic naturally causing my employer fear and worry of the baby contracting the virus, and also because as a new comer, I couldn't be trusted.

I was watched by security cameras for everything I did. This was to continue even after I had proved myself a trustworthy person, and it remained in place permanently going forward for whoever entered their home thereafter.

Salomon Estate, situated close by, was a stunning Victorian mansion situated just outside the genteel spa-town of Royal Tunbridge Wells where I now lived. Set in 36 acres of gardens, parkland and woods, the estate was built for Sir David Salomons in the 1850s by the architect Decimus Burton. Born in 1797, Sir David Salomons, 1st Baronet, was a leading figure in the 19th century struggle for Jewish emancipation in the United kingdom.

He was the first Jewish sheriff of the city of London and Lord Mayor of London. Today, the house is a hotel, museum and visitors' centre. My employers' home had originally been farm buildings belongings to the estate but now had been turned into executive homes with access to the hotel grounds. This was the only place I was allowed out with the baby and we would spend my days walking and exploring the glorious stunning grounds for an hour twice a day and then returning to my employers' home.

Soon after working for her, I started to randomly hear gunshot fire and shouting on the grounds of the hotel which naturally alarmed me. My employer told me that journalists and war correspondents were on courses being trained in journalist warfare. This did not stop the baby and me doing our regular daily perambulations through the grounds, as it was the only place we were allowed out at that time.

While doing this on one occasion, I shockingly found myself walking past a re-enactment of a situation they were having. I saw a man dressed as an Afghan soldier with a long black beard and army clothing holding a Kalashnikov rifle, standing next to a Land Rover vehicle shouting to a group of people. It was a surprising scene to see in such a beautiful and peaceful part of middle England and because of that, it exaggerated the impact.

They were blocking my way and as I pushed past them with the pram, I joked to alleviate the tension I witnessed and said to them that this could be an ordinary every day event happening as an innocent bystander found themselves in the wrong place at the wrong time.

Later on, my way back from our walk, the guy leading the course, who was ex-army, had come up to me and was friendly, telling me that the re-enactment was of a child just having been run over by the Land Rover at a check point and that the journalists thought I was part of the re-enactment. We proceeded to have an interesting discussion and I talked about Andy Mcnabs' book, *Trauma,* and the experiences he had in the SAS.

I asked the course leader if he had seen action, which of course he had. He told me it was just a job to him and said nothing more on the subject. I knew quite a different story from his 'brothers in arms' when I had met an ex-army soldier who had come to my little cottage in Stanton in the Cotswolds when I lived there as a handyman to help fix something in my home and who had seen me reading Andy Mcnabs' book, *Trauma*, at the time and started engaging in conversation.

Andy talks about the armed forces and how only recently in the last 20 years had the armed forces recognised and acknowledged PTSD in soldiers who had come out of combat deployment.

Soldiers who had come out of service in the past were having a hard time readjusting to life outside the military. Not being able to cope with life after war had been classed in the past by the armed forces as a weakness, Lilly livered and cowardly. Even today, soldiers are not getting the treatment follow-up they need and are only supported with minimal adequate care.

Post-traumatic stress disorder, sometimes known as shell shock or combat stress, occurs after you experience severe trauma or a life threatening event. It is normal for your mind and body to be in shock after such an event, but this normal response becomes PTSD when your nervous system gets 'stuck'.

Mobilisation, or fight or flight, occurs when you need to defend yourself or survive the danger of a combat situation— your heart pounds faster, your blood pressure rises, and your muscles tighten, increasing your strength and reaction speed. Once the danger has passed, your body lowers your heart rate and blood pressure, and winds back down to its normal balance.

Immobilisation occurs when you've experienced too much stress in a situation and even though the danger has passed, you find yourself 'stuck'. Your nervous system is unable to return to its normal state of balance and you're unable to move on from the event. This is PTSD.

Soldiers can develop this in hours or days following a traumatic event; sometimes symptoms don't surface for months or even years after return from deployment. Symptoms can develop differently in each veteran with four symptom clusters—recurrent, intrusive reminders of the traumatic event, including distressing thoughts, nightmares, and flashbacks where you feel like the event is happening again.

They may experience extreme emotional and physical reactions to reminders of the trauma such as panic attacks, uncontrollable shaking, and heart palpitations.

Extreme avoidance of things that remind them of the traumatic event, including people, places, thoughts, or situations that are associated with the bad memories. This can include withdrawals from friends and family and losing interest in everyday activities. Negative changes in mood and thought, such as exaggerated negative beliefs about yourself or the world and persistent feelings of fear guilt or shame. There may be a diminished ability to experience positive emotions.

Being on guard all the time and jumpy and emotionally reactive, as indicated by irritation, anger, reckless behaviour, difficulties sleeping, trouble concentrating, and increased alertness.

The ex-veteran and I had sat down together at my cottage and despite being total strangers had a very interesting and frank conversation, where he opened up to me about his post-traumatic stress disorder and how his experiences of coming out of the army into civil-street was a very difficult transition indeed. He told me that while serving in Afghanistan, he had seen 10 year old Afghan boys decapitate British soldiers without any emotion or remorse.

He told me that every time he heard a car backfire or fireworks go off, he suffered recall and went into defence mode. He told me that his wife was very supportive but was finding his dreams and nightmares hard to live with.

I had given him the book to keep and he had taken it away with him. As an HSP and having experienced my own trauma of losing my son and suffering recurring PTSD symptoms throughout my life time from the cruel psychological treatment and emotional abuse that I had received from the people who were supposed to of loved me, including my childhood experiences, we had connected on a level of understanding of each other's pain and suffering.

I had experienced and therefore had come to accept that life is hard and in our lifetime, sometimes we will be surrounded by people who just do not have it in them to treat us properly, which is never an easy thing to deal with at the time. The important thing is how we get ourselves away from those people, and take back and regain our lives, thoughts and trust.

The pain and trauma they induced will permanently stay in our memories, but the challenge is not to keep revisiting them. Healing takes time, so does forgiveness, and as for the pain and suffering, it never leaves us sadly, although we move past it just enough to be able to move forward in our lives. Professional help and counselling are also required to be able to do this affectively.

It is tempting, therefore, to treat people the same way as we have been treated but it takes great work on oneself to still treat people kindly despite what we have been through. This is what makes a beautiful person. It is their ability to show kindness and understanding amongst their hurt, pain and suffering.

If you are willing to take a look at another person's behaviour towards you as a reflection of the state of their relationship with themselves rather than your value as a person, then you will, over a period of time, cease to react at all.

As for the soldier, well that was a different Trauma for him to overcome and it would need specialist psychological treatment to help him recover from his war experiences and the responsibility of the British Army to see that he got the support he so clearly needed. So why do some people experience such things and others not? The army course leader at the hotel certainly had not. Research suggests that soldiers cope with their combat deployment differently depending on what goes back to childhood.

If a child experienced trauma in their early years, by the time that person is around the ages of early adulthood through to their mid-30s, it will impact them so severely. If you look at the studies on post-traumatic stress disorder, 100 soldiers that go into battle, 20 that go home with PTSD are the people with traumatising childhood; the adult experience simply triggers the old trauma.

It is said that in concentration camp survivors, those who had safe, supportive early childhoods had a much better chance of coming out of it without significant trauma symptoms. When our brains are formed in childhood that is when our personalities form and our fundamental beliefs about the world are formed and we develop either positive or negative attitudes towards ourselves, towards our possibilities.

Later on in life, how we deal with adversity is very much conditioned by how we were raised in the first place. My experiences working with children as a nanny and care giver and also my own childhood experiences made me very much aware of this.

After this experience, my employer, not knowing anything about my recent encounter on the grounds of the hotel, herself would send me articles on my phone on statistics of child abductions and health scares such as children swallowing batteries and accidents in the home; indeed the lady surgeon had conducted operations to remove such things herself.

She was a very negative and fearful person, always focusing on the dreadful and inhuman side of life. I did not like being around this kind of energy as my spiritual belief system believed that you attracted what you feared. I kindly and politely told her that these things happened to a very minor percentage of the population and that only real positive vibes were required for us. Her husband agreed with me and soon restrictions were reduced.

Still there were challenges, understandably as the reins were loosened, and I needed to report where and when I went out and was also required to send her photographs via my mobile phone while I was out and about to show I was where I was supposed to be. I was an automaton in nature and therefore, this went against my natural way of functioning and conducting myself. Still, I persevered knowing there are lessons to learn in everything.

I very soon found myself being asked to come in early for work and my day soon began at 6.20am in the mornings taking me through to 7pm, with overtime at the weekends. The money was good and gave myself and my daughter financial security and my new employer would compliment me on being a super nanny to her 9 month old child and how lucky they were to have me. But after a while, the pressure of supporting this family became too much.

I was pretty much cooking all the family meals each week. They wanted to move to a bigger house next door and one weekend I was asked to come in on my day off and look after the sweet little boy while this happened.

I had been asked to re-seed the garden lawn where bald patches had occurred due to toys and garden furniture being kept on it and when the weekend in question arrived, I ended up actually moving their belongings into the new home and installing them in their correct place, while also running errands for them while the baby slept. It seemed my employer was becoming more demanding by the day. I had now also been asked if I could iron her husband's shirts.

I liked keeping busy as it helped the day pass quickly, but I was soon to find there was no break time in a 12-hour day, and this cumulative effect after three months, my age at 58 years old and the early morning starts and extra demands, soon began to affect my health. So I decided I had no choice other than to quit my job as I became physically unable to do it.

By the time the little boy had reached 12 months old, he had already had three different nannies looking after him on a full-time basis.

It started to dawn on me that this new generation of parents without the support of grandparents and other family members, who required full-time childcare so that they could work, were quite happy to pay and allow someone else to effectively run their homes and raise their children. Parents loved their children but I was beginning to wonder why people had children in the first place when they spent so little time with them.

In the three years of being a nanny, I started to see patterns of behaviour in the children I was looking after. I had a huge amount of love to give and so would support the children whenever they felt anxious or sad, and I had always approached children with a sentiment of tenderness for what they were and respect for what they may become.

I was a feminist and supported women's rights to have careers and financial independence, but I was seeing the emotional impact that this was having on their children as they were suffering the ill effects of time-poor parents. Babies from birth to age three were showing signs of becoming withdrawn, compliant and sad, and in some cases, showing signs of aggression and I felt sorry for them.

Parents would share with me in a prideful way the 5-star nurseries that their babies would be on the waiting lists for. They were happy to put their babies in nursery as young as 8 weeks old onwards. Some of these nurseries offered hot croissant and coffees in reception each morning for anyone who wanted to grab breakfast while on the move.

The kids' lunches where high-end menus such as teriyaki salmon and restaurant-quality food (this was Royal Tunbridge Wells of course) the parents would tell me in an exuberant manner as if to justify their actions why they were putting their children into care so young. But I just saw a replacement of care other than their mother's. Because their children were left in luxury, it somehow justified parents effectively abandoning their children at such a young age.

The UK has more than 450,000 children in nursery care. The world had gone completely mad I felt.

Parents, it seemed, were having trouble with the day-to-day management of their own children and their homes while having to hold down their full-time jobs; the pressure/ stress was too much for them and they couldn't cope it seemed. On weekends when parents should have been resting from their busy working week, they had to manage their children and life admin.

I noticed that this was a strain on them. Therefore, more often than not, I was asked to come in on weekends to help out by extending my working week. I could see that the children were desperately missing that time spent with their parents, which I felt terribly sad about. I worried that this was causing a kind of PDSD (Prolonged Duress Stress Disorder) effect on the children with their needs from their parents not being met.

Later, I was to find out that the cost of ownership of a home in the south east of England was so expensive that it required two incomes to be able to afford to buy and maintain a house, and therefore, somewhat explained the parents' dilemma. Also, the cost of raising a child in the UK at this time was estimated between £150,000 and £200,000, this included housing and childcare costs. That is around £10,000 a year or £800 a month.

I remember my own mother telling me that when I was a baby and when dad was building his business, she didn't own a washing machine and had to wash our clothes in the bath. Indeed, when my children were young, I couldn't afford a tumble dryer and so wet clothes would hang on radiators around the house, but at least we were around for our children.

It seems that everyone these days must have the best of everything without waiting and that to provide, it meant work work work, and certainly our country is benefiting hugely economically from women going back to work straight after they've had their babies. In terms of the happiness and wellbeing of our children, I felt we were at a crossroads.

With this economic pressure on parents clearly visible to me, I was also witnessing first hand more and more children showing ADHD symptoms. The neurologist and physician Dr Gabor Mate, who has a background in family practice and a special interest in childhood development, wrote the book *Scattered Minds*, where he describes Attention Deficit Disorder or ADHD as a reversible impairment and a developmental delay with the origins in infancy.

Rather than a medical illness, he describes how it can be reversible and that while there may be a genetic predisposition, it can be cured.

He describes it as rooted in multigenerational family stress and in disturbed social conditions in a stressed society. Originated in early childhood with stresses during the first years of crucial brain and personality development, this causes symptoms such as frequent, involuntary and frustrating tuning-out or absent of mind, difficulties concentrating unless very interested in something, being bored easily, beginning one thing but going on to another before completion of the first task.

Difficulty in being on time, and poor impulse control, manifested in speaking out of turn, and interrupting others in conversation. Impulse buying and addictive behaviour and physical hyperactivity, especially in males, difficulties in sitting still, and fidgeting. Temperamentally and highly sensitive.

He describes how the child's environment can be improved by looking at the internal and external stress in the family and the quality of the relationships the child is surrounded by. He asks us to look at the amount of structure and security that the family environment provides. When something is slightly off in the surroundings, for example, stresses in the marriage relationship. ADHD children are highly sensitive and these things can trip emotional alarms much more readily than other children.

The statistics today show that one in nine people suffer from the condition compared to in the 1980s when one in twenty children suffered from ADHD. The parenting environment that I was witnessing was becoming a much more stressed environment in today's society causing these statistics.

Raising a child requires unconditional love, consistency, clear guidance and endless giving. It also requires a watchful eye, endless patience, thoughtful teaching, careful role modelling, a listening ear, a fair mind and an open heart. Raising a child is the most beautiful gift. The foundation of who that child will become is determined by his parents, his family and his surroundings.

Over the past 40 years, I have raised my own children and have been a stay at home mum. This was my choice even though my husband at the time had wanted me to work outside of the home and contribute to the family finances. I refused to do this because I wanted to be there for them in every way possible that a mother could be, and therefore, we had to adjust the finances accordingly, which meant going without certain things.

The UK has seen an almost continual rise in the proportion of women in employment. The employment rate amount women of 'prime working age' (25-54) was up from 57% in 1975 to a record high of 78% in 2017. This predominantly reflected an increase in full-time employment from 29% in 1985 (when data of hours began) to 44% in 2017. The UK economy, therefore, looks dramatically different today from how it did back in the 1970s.

One of the most striking changes in the labour market is the increased share of women in employment and one of the dramatically looking differences today is the dramatic effect on the raising of children in the home.

I would have to take children to doctors and health visitor appointments, sometimes the parent would forget and I would have to stand in not really knowing much about the child's medical history because I had just started the job. I could see the doctors' and health workers' uncomfortable demeanour as someone other than the child's parents answered personal questions about the child; in fact, I was surprised that this was allowed.

From personal experience, I knew that doctors themselves put their own children into nurseries because I had been contacted on the childcare website by hospital doctors asking if I was available to collect their children from nursery and take them home. It was common for pre-schoolers to be in a nursery from 7.30am to 6.30pm five days a week.

What was becoming of us as a society? It seemed that nurture was slowly becoming non-existent. Was this the new way forward as humanity changed towards its new environment. Was I witnessing history changing family dynamics before my eyes? It seemed that this, in part, must be due to women now cohabiting and having children both less frequently and later in life.

The share of women living with a partner or spouse by age 25 had fallen from more than 80% for women born in the

1940s to less than 60% for women born in the 1970s, while the share of women born in 1975 who had given birth to at least one child by age 25 (31%) was around half that of women born in 1945 (60%) according to statistics.

Overall, the proportion of working-age mothers in paid work was up from 50% in 1975 to 72% in 2015. The rise had been particularly large among lone mothers and mothers of pre-school and primary-school age children.

I was spending 75 hours a week at this point in time with these children, effectively raising them with my values, morals disciplines and core beliefs. At least the children I looked after had me as a consistent one-on-one carer who attended to their emotional needs, and who gave guidance and sympathy, whereas those children in nurseries were getting intertutionised from such a very early age with instruction and probably only had their physical needs met.

This was a huge undertaking for me, especially if the parents' values differed from my own. In childhood, a child's development is a period of physical, cognitive and social growth that begins at birth and continues right through to early adulthood. These types of developmental milestones cover both physical and psychological changes that children undergo. But these goals can be heavily influenced by internal and external factors.

Indeed, my own 15 year old daughter had to fend for herself as my days started early and ended late. I was too tired to cook dinner when I got home from work and she would have to cook for herself or eat a takeaway meal. I couldn't keep an eye on her social or mental health at this time, especially given that the teenage years were a tricky time anyway.

Was I witnessing the downfall of the nuclear family unit as we know it in the UK? My daughter's father lived one and a half hours away and was unavailable on a regular basis to help out and release the pressure of raising a teenager.

I wondered how this would affect the children psychologically going forward as they became adults. Would they be full of resentment and anger as they looked back at their childhoods, or would they find coping mechanisms that would eventually surface in adulthood and compromise their own relationships?

Also with so many different strangers/ caregivers looking after them in their childhood, what psychological imprints would have been conditioned in them and how would that impact them in adulthood? The social relationships that a child has can be hugely impactful, so thinking about who they have regular access to and how that influences them is hugely important.

Being surrounded by loving, nurturing, safe individuals is the key. Children are like sponges. They pick up on everything, so we have to be mindful of who and what they are surrounded by. The quality of their interactions with others will determine their intellectual, social and emotional development.

Women, it seemed, were much less likely to drop out of the labour market nowadays, especially around the time they had their first child, and much more likely to stay in paid work, whereby women of my mother's generation were less likely to still be in work, things were definitely changing.

I wanted to get away from the childcare sector for these reasons because of what I was witnessing did not sit comfortably with me and it upset me enormously. The pandemic had caused some parents to work from home and this made the nannying job twice as difficult.

Many people preferred (or simply couldn't avoid) this arrangement. There were many perks, conveniences, safety, and abilities to maintain proximity to their children, but while this was very convenient for the parents, it made things very stressful for the nanny. In fact, many nannies would not accept these types of positions because it often made the days 'more difficult'.

Nannies develop a routine in the home, ideally, we have strategies and rules, time tables and goals. I would plan transitions from one activity to the next to avoid meltdowns, to increase learning and to provide positive social interactions.

This routine took time to establish and sticking to it was crucial to a successful day but when you work from the parents' home, them popping in and out would interrupt this routine. The children would get easily off track from homework, naps, snacks/ meals, etc., and the parents surfacing for a coffee or a hello would cause meltdowns from the children because ultimately they preferred being with their parents.

I more often than not would be left to pick up the pieces as they exited. Also, it didn't feel right stopping a child from going to be with their parents.

Knowing their parents were tucked away in a room in the home also made the day difficult by stopping the children from going into the room where their parents were trying to work. In an open planned home, this was impossible. I was starting to dislike being effectively in a stranger's home who you didn't know, and there was always a risk of walking into a chaotic dysfunctional and unsafe environment.

In fact, I had heard one 4 year old little boy say to his father 'don't hit me'. I felt that DBS checks, which were a mandatory requirement for nannies, should also be a requirement for parents of children in some of the homes I was working in.

The royalties from my book would have taken a while to come through so I couldn't give up my day job just yet, so I proceeded to look for more work. I took on interim work for a while but the nature of short contracts at that time meant I was constantly looking for new work and the anxiety that entailed was stressful. I was solely responsible for the roof over my daughter's head and financially, it was all down to me.

In September that same year, soon after I had resigned from my job, I caught the Corona Virus. I was not surprised as I was so overworked and run down in health. My daughter, Summer, myself and Paul, her father, had gone on a vacation break for a couple of days to Oxford and then onto the Welsh Marshes area, and somewhere during those travels, I had contracted it. Thankfully by then, I had been vaccinated twice and so even though very unpleasant, I had survived it.

Paul and I continued to remain friends despite our separation 2 years earlier and we would spend the odd times together with our daughter whenever possible. I had forgiven my ex-husband for all the terrible things he had done to me in the past. I know some of you who know the background to my story will wonder why. Why does she still continue to have a relationship with someone who inflicted such chaos, pain and bad things, surely she must have a clear mental and emotional image in her unconscious mind of who he is.

All the things that had accumulated over the years with him were not pleasant I agree, surely those things must still live in her, so why would she still want to be around him? Well, the answer is that I had learnt through my spiritual teachings not to go into a reactive mode when around him and not be triggered by old habits of thinking. I had to be really really present in the moments I spent with him without the past.

We had shared a lot of unpleasant things together and the past had been difficult, but it had also been littered with success, and while it was worth letting go of the heavy parts, it was still beneficial to hold onto the productive ones. We also shared some wonderful and incredible experiences and, more importantly, we shared a child. I was finally able to meet him without reference to the negatives of the past.

Once I understood how to do this, I had the ability to meet another human being that way because of the real forgiveness I was able to achieve by being fully in the present. That is how far I had come in my awakening. Sometimes, not always, but through this practice, it is sufficient unto itself that there can be a miraculous transformation in the other person if you meet them and not reference the past.

If we want change, then we need to free the other person from their heavy personality. When one of the two people in the relationship becomes conscious, it can free the other. This was freedom on my account as I did not want to carry around with me an unpleasant emotional mental entity living within me. Some people actually like harbouring grievances or long-standing resentment as the ego can hold on to it, but by doing that we are never truly free, only bitter.

I understood that the betrayal he had inflicted on me had nothing to do with me. It had to do with his own pain, his own coping mechanisms, his trauma and his dysfunction. It didn't make it any easier being on the receiving end of this, but once he had revealed a very broken side to himself, it showed me that it literally had nothing to do with me and I was able, therefore, not to not take it personally anymore.

Here was a very hurt, lost person who was coping with that loss in an incredibly destructive way. I had empathy for that. His behaviour did not, in any way, determine whether or not I was a loveable person, and it had nothing to do with me.

Towards the end of the year, near Christmas time, I managed to secure a position as a PA/ nanny role for parents who had their own online business and I was employed by their company as an executive assistant. The job came with a private healthcare package and extras. Their little boy was starting school at nursery and I was to do the school runs and manage his activities out of school while managing their home, admin and the cooking of healthy meals.

The job would take on more of a PA role as the little boy started full-time school the following September which I felt was more of a career move at the time. It would see me through to the next chapter of my life while my books were being published and I could move more into alinement with my true calling.

Sadly, after only two weeks on the job, I was presented with an aggressive dysfunctional family whereby I had no choice other than to leave. I felt very uncomfortable in the presence of the father of the young boy, who was Glaswegian;

his manners were aggressive, dominant and overbearing. I also felt he was a misogynist.

The parents both worked from home and I tried to have a calm conversation with him on the practicalities of keeping his son from disturbing their working day as he continually was trying to enter their home office. Given it was an open-plan house without doors, I constantly had to remove the child from wanting to be with his parents, to the point of physically restraining the child.

I felt uncomfortable doing this, and with a child of 5 years of age, who was heavy and consistently fighting against me, I had consequently put my back out. I tried, therefore, to take the little boy outside to parks and recreational spaces as much as possible but this had been commented on as being too frequent.

We had a discussion about this situation but no alternative plans could be agreed upon. On further discussion, when I had calmly fought my ground and said that I could not possibly work under such circumstances, the father had accused me of being hysterical, which I certainly had not been. He had gaslighted me. Sigmund Freud invented the word hysteria back in his day, opposed to women's emancipation movement and with a view that they were dominated by their sexual reproductive functions.

He coined the word because he was focused on the belief that the very presence of a uterus must cause the symptoms of neurosis. It had been a derogatory remark towards me as a woman, and therefore, it had been a sexist remark. He did not like my assertiveness, the rejection of me quitting the job and proceeded to insult me.

Nowadays, every time I got disillusioned by someone or something, I felt liberated because I had control. I was not afraid of disillusionment anymore because it meant that I was able to look at reality in the face and not be afraid to sense the truth of it, even if it was painful or disruptive. I had heard the little boy on one occasion say 'don't hit me' to his father and this had sent off huge alarm bells in me. I could not work with such a person, and therefore, promptly left.

I now knew from the past that stress came from the way I reacted to things and not the way life is. If I adjusted my attitude and changed how I saw things, then all the extra stress, worrying and overthinking could go away.

The body has powerful consciousness and is continually using its whole system to help guide our lives and the energy in them. The nervous system communicates through energetics, vibration, emotions, and signals. Are we honouring those signals? They come to guide us towards higher vibrations and not away from them.

Those feelings of butterflies in the pit of your stomach are not a sign of high vibrational attraction but unsettledness and alarm. When you are at ease around balanced people, you are disarmed and there is no fight or flight mode.

The right people induce the right neurotransmitters (chemical messengers) in our body which will calm us. Sometimes these feelings can be mistaken as 'boring' or 'boredom' or 'too normal' if you are used to the feeling of butterflies, chaotic, and flight or fight relationships energy, like I had been.

As you drop into the mindful practice of honouring the best relational and energetic connections for you and your nervous system, the sense of boredom will transform into a safe, calm, joyous and high vibrational relationship energy. These types of relationships, working or personal, will fulfil and reward you in long-term in ways that a low vibrational one could never.

It is important to listen to your body for your health and honour the wisdom within; the process of honouring who and what is good for you and your nervous system. The right people will feel different to your nervous system.

I had spent a lifetime in the past ignoring my own needs and abandoning myself for the sake of others. I had tolerated poor behaviour and had 'put up' with other people's dysfunction for so long, that I was not prepared for this to happen to me anymore. My life's journey had taught me so much that I wasn't allowing my nervous system to suffer any longer. I now looked at each situation I came across as a lesson and a new opportunity to grow.

With this in mind, it prompted me to take a long hard look at my career choices and I started to see that I had leadership qualities, and therefore, I bravely decided to go the self-employed route where I would be in control of who I chose to work for and the job would not control me. I decided to do it on an ad-hoc basis, whereby I would have flexibility and variation within the jobs I took on.

Hopefully, I will be able to be more discerning when picking and choosing who I want to work with and not panic and take the wrong role out of financial pressure. The childcare website that I signed up with was now showing huge demand for nannies in my area, so much so that the demand now outweighed the availability. With this in mind and the knowledge that what I had to offer was very marketable things, it would finally be on my own terms.

I was starting to be so much more intuitive and if the vibes were not organic, I would walk away. If the energy felt off, then I would leave it alone. If my spirit did not want it, then I didn't resist the rejection. By forcing my way through each chapter, I was only creating more delays, more obstacles, and more roadblocks to appear in my path. By following my way through my journey, I was aligning myself with the right people, the right opportunities, and the right doors to walk through.

I understand now that growth requires us to leave something behind. It can be our habits, beliefs, careers, mindset, and even people. And this is why making space for grief in the midst of growth is important. You may mourn your former life to make space for a newer you. I am always curious as to why some of us face a challenge with change.

We know certain behaviour is unhealthy; maybe some of us haven't really accepted we can change at all, especially when we see the consequences in our lives and the impact on other people. maybe our relationship ends. Maybe we go through a lot of challenges and we are told that we are the source of it, or that we are part of it. Sometimes, obviously, there is no truth in it and someone just wants to point the finger, but often or not, there is truth in the feedback we are given, especially the outcomes.

We are the common denominators of all the outcomes in our lives. So we explore why that thing did not work, or why that outcome I want I'm not achieving; why am I not engaging in actual change? What's getting in the way?

I was starting to feel I needed to explore how I earned my living. I definitely felt unsuited anymore being in a full-time employed position. I was not prepared to accept being taken advantage of by my employers because they had overstretched themselves and were time-deprived, therefore placing more responsibility on me. This was becoming a familiar pattern in all the positions I had undertaken thus far.

Again that dreadful feeling of exploitation would kick in and I definitely was not having that again. I also was seeing in me the need to accommodate people based on the need to be liked and to keep the peace, something I had done all my life until this point. I am a kind person and sometimes this was taken advantage of, so I started to explore the idea of things like intuition and feeling connected to the divine, feeling connected to soul and feeling connected to self. This was terribly important to me.

Do you know how much energy it takes to walk into a job that you cannot stand, and yet, most of us do it every day. Instead of resisting, imagine if we just redirected some of that energy towards looking for something else, like the leaves falling from a tree. You make a decision that today I am going to let go of the talking and complaining about this because that is the exact energy that zaps me.

Direct the energy instead at something positive, because once we get rid of that, we have room for something positive to grow. If we are arguing against our god given potential, we are actively destroying our confidence and possibilities.

What I did know was that on this journey of mine, I was trying to discover that, and exploring how I know when I'm in alinement. Well, I definitely know when I'm not, and these nannying jobs where the employer was in charge trying to micromanage me and demanding more of my time were starting to show me this. Also, these were new inexperienced parents and usually, they didn't know what they were doing.

I had 40 years of childcare experience and expertise and was not going to be told how to do something by someone who evidently didn't have a clue what they were doing but had an ego that said otherwise. This thinking was behind my decision to go out on a limb and run my own ad-hoc childcare business.

One of the hardest truths I learnt at this stage in my life journey was that you cannot count on anyone or anything, no matter who they are to you, or how well you think you know someone. Anyone can disappoint, abandon, betray, or devastate you. Your spouse/ partner, your parents, even your own children. There are stories aplenty, including my own, where all these things have happened.

Once you have lived through a few such experiences, the truth of 'free will' and human nature becomes painfully apparent. Not everyone keeps loyalty and empathy as personal commitments, and sometimes even we fail ourselves; therefore, I had to find my own independence and be reliant on myself.

What I do know is that it felt lighter. I felt liberated; I felt safer. I felt I loved who I was becoming because of the choices I was making. Even if those choices were scary at first and caused disruption, or other people's feelings were being impacted, somehow I felt I was good and I've got me, not putting other people's feelings ahead of my own. Which doesn't mean I was not considerate of other people feelings or aware of the impact I was having on other people's choices.

That's when I knew I was in alinement with who I truly was. Our lives can become prisons of choices we made decades ago and then we don't change or move forward. The employed nanny route had been a good decision initially to help me with my independence and financial security after leaving my husband.

Through this route initially, I had discovered a creative side to myself while having worked for my lovely creative work family. They opened me up to the writing of my books, which consequently opened up a portal in me where the desire to write was a shift so strong, that in spare time I continued to write. I would not stay stuck in past ways of behaviour of doing things. Life is transient and change is inevitable and we must push forward if we are to evolve.

A polite reminder to you, dear reader, that at the end of your life, which by the way could come at any moment, all that will matter to you is: Did you love with all your heart? Did you have boundaries? Did you live a life that was true to you? Did you live a life in true alinement and integrity with your values? That is what will truly matter most. At any moment, you can just decide to change and get into alinement with those things.

You will realise that in the relationships where you don't feel like you can't be you, you are choosing to participate in them, the habits, the rituals, the choices you're making day in and day out, that you think you have to make because you have no other choice, let me tell you that you do have another choice. And you'll notice that in hindsight when you get to death's door. But why wait for that? You can do it with foresight on the way.

You can get to death's door and look back and say 'That was the moment when I changed; that was the moment I was in true alinement'.

Chapter 2

Time passed and my new business was thriving. I had now been independently living on my own for nearly 3 years and managing financially, something that most people take for granted these days and do automatically without any real thought towards it. Due to my background and childhood experiences of low self-esteem, I had chosen to have children at a young age and raise them at home and not work outside of it.

This caused me to be solely dependent on others, mainly my husbands for my livelihood. Therefore, it was a massive achievement of financial independence to have finally reached this point. At times, it still embarrassed me that it had taken 40 years to achieve this. A whole new experience for me. I guess the beauty of life is that while we can't undo what is done, we can see it, understand it, learn from it, and change so that every new moment is spent not in regret, guilt, fear or anger but in wisdom, understanding and love.

One day out of the blue, I found myself a little lonely for male company and intimacy with someone to share the day-to-day struggles and nice things in life with. Although, I received love from the children I looked after, and also from my daughters, I was missing romantic grown-up love and affection.

With everything I had been through with my past two marriages that had failed miserably, I was consistently following experts' and therapists' advice on social media for the healing of past wounds in these relationships and also embracing the latest dating trends.

The more I dived into the work of understanding relationships, communication, how to get better, how to change my life, how to show up, and how to deal with it all, I believed that so much of it was connected to our nervous system, especially understanding our biology and unstuckness. I knew that I truly wanted great love and that I could truly create a beautiful relationship, and not just romantically but a beautiful life. I knew that cognitively, but it's funny how we can sometimes choose everything but that.

In the past, I had allowed self-limiting beliefs to never let myself succeed and I had self-sabotaged myself and never let myself get anywhere (I explain how this happened in my first book, *The Journey*). None of that seemed logical now as no one would rationally do that. No one would stay in an abusive relationship; no one would keep themselves small or not use their voice; but I had.

There is so much beyond what happens in the unconscious mind and in our bodies, that we don't know it's happening. I didn't even know, for instance, especially when I was young and growing up, that the chaos and dysregulation of my childhood weren't normal. I didn't even know I was co-dependant and dysregulated, but it was my normal. Then through my life experiences and healing process and the writing of my memoirs, I became regulated.

And now it was like 'what the heck', it's so calm and peaceful, which was what I was feeling at that moment in time after so much trauma in my past behind me. I felt the time was good to embark on a healthy relationship.

I had not dated anyone in 23 years and the thought of presenting myself to the world as an available single person was daunting, to say the least. I was a totally different person now. I had healed myself from my past traumas. My journey had taught me so much and so I now possessed personal boundaries.

I could recognise negative behaviour patterns. I was a lot more discerning and could spot red flags when they arose, and therefore, I felt ready to meet a love interest again. I was determined I was not going to make the same mistakes I had made before in my previous relationships.

In early January 2021 and coming out of lockdown after much research, I decided to employ a personal matchmaker believing a professional matchmaking service would do a good job of finding me love. I proceeded to go through the elite formal proceedings to enrol on their books. They had to do security checks on me and ascertain I was a bonafide person and did not suffer any mental health issues or was in any way a criminal.

I had professional photographs taken and an interview with my personal assigned matchmaker where many questions were asked and a profile of myself was drawn up. A very formal outfit with a huge cost associated with it. I felt it was an investment in a hugely important part of my future, a partner who would be handpicked for me and matched to my personality type. The Myers-Briggs method was used.

The purpose of the Myer-Briggs Type Indicator personality inventory was to make the theory of psychological types described by C. G. Jung understandable and useful in people's lives. The essence of the theory is that many random variations in the behaviour is actually quite orderly and consistent, being due to basic differences in the ways individuals prefer to use their perception and judgement.

Perception involves all the ways of becoming aware of things, people, happenings, or ideas. Judgement involves all the ways of coming to conclusions about what has been perceived. Apparently, if people differ systematically in what they perceive and how they reach conclusions, then it is only reasonable for them to differ correspondingly in their interests, reactions, values, motivations, and skills.

In developing the Myer-Briggs Type Indicator, the aim of Isabel Briggs Myers and her mother, Katharine Briggs, was to make insights of type theory accessible to individuals and groups. They addressed the two related goals in the development and application of the MBTI instrument.

I had been tested and my type was determined as an ENFJ personality type. Often called the protagonist, a person with extroverted intuitive feelings and judging traits. Warm and forthright, we love helping others and tend to have strong ideas and values. We back our perspective with the creative energy to achieve our goals.

Called to serve a greater purpose in life, thoughtful and idealistic, we strive to have a positive impact on others and the world around us. We rarely shy away from an opportunity to do the right thing, even when doing so is far from easy.

I couldn't afford the six introductions that the agency offered, my nannying salary would not stretch that far and so feeling confident, I signed up for the discounted price of three introductions. I felt excited at the thought of new beginnings and meetings some interesting people who had been personally selected for me. My first introduction was with a well-known artist living in Belgravia in London.

A very good-looking Jewish fellow and the same age as myself. We spoke briefly on the phone and arranged to meet up at his home on Cundy street in London for dinner. We were both excited that we had been professionally matched and in anticipation, I wore a feminine and pretty blue summer dress and high heels for the occasion.

I was to drive to London after a full day of work to meet him at his home. After a 2-hour journey, I arrived and was met by him at the gates of his exclusive address. Standing over 6ft tall, he was slim and very handsome, and I couldn't help but feel excited and hopeful. I had done my own due diligence online and already knew he was well-known within his industry, successful and mixing in the Echelons of high society.

I had seen pictures of him on social media and in newspapers with beautiful famous actresses, including show cases of his art work.

Once inside his apartment, despite the impressive address, I was shocked and appalled to find an overcrowded small 'run down at heal' flat full of rubbish lying everywhere. Piles of newspapers, books, pictures. His gold leaf art work was mounted randomly and carelessly on the walls and floor. The bathroom furniture was chipped and stained and looked ancient like a student's squat full of squalor and decay.

Despite all this, I was made to feel that I was honoured to be in his company and was told that I could stay and that I would do nicely. As he asked me to sit down on the old sofa, the cushions of which were so old I could feel the metal spring digging into me and any hope of getting back up from the sofa in quick succession was probably out of the question.

Once pleasantries were out of the way, he was keen to serve dinner. He was a good cook and delivered a nice fish meal. Sadly, I couldn't finish it as I was so nervous and on my guard because I had this uneasy feeling. So he said he would save the leftovers for his dinner the following day. For the rest of the evening, I had to fend off his amorous advances and at one point, he literally tried to climb on top of me!

He had mentioned that he did not like my strong, confident, independent and capable manner, and commented on the fact that I needed taking in hand. I laugh as I write this memory but the truth was, at the time, I felt frightened and vulnerable and rather stupid agreeing to meet at his home. Basically, he was a leech and expected sex on demand. I felt I had been treated like a call girl.

Afterwards, I complained to the agency and told them I could, in fact, sue him for molestation because his behaviour had been so appalling and improper, and literally, threatening. The experience had been so shocking. Their reply was that some couples do have sex on the first date, so they were relaxed and took no further action.

Some months later, I was to find out that his residence was due for demolition because it was outdated and run down. His building was knocked down to make way for a new luxury-apartment development and he had been rehoused in a new residence in Chelsea. The dating agency had refused him any more introductions and had banned him from using their dating site as it transpired that he was somewhat of an odd character. My first experience of the dating scene had been a disaster.

The next couple of dates were less stressful and although very interesting and successful men, I did begin to wonder why they wanted companionship in the first place, considering they were so busy and successful in their chosen profession that they did not appear to have the time to invest in a relationship. I had to sign a couple of NDAs before meeting these men, so unfortunately, I can't relay my experiences in this book.

Suffice to say, they would have made very interesting reading indeed. All I can tell you is that one of the gentlemen in question shockingly had associations with the Fred West Murders; his ex-wife had been one of Rose and Fred West's daughters. I did not find the love and connection I was seeking and felt my considerable financial investment had been a waste of money.

My last attempt at a love connection was helped by the Malaysian employer while I was still working for her. She could see each day via her security system camera that on the rare breaks I had, I was online watching relationship experts on how to find love. Without asking me, she had explored and set up an online dating site for me that she felt would offer me a better introduction to men. She herself had met her partner on an online dating site.

Apparently, when she had told her colleagues at work that she was doing this for me, they advised her that she was overstepping professional boundaries, but she was a kind person who cared about me and so went ahead anyway. All I had to do was pay the subscription and when she told me she had done this, I was grateful and appreciative.

In July 2021, I met a nice gentleman from Oxford who was a quantity surveyor from my employer's recommended dating website, who also held his own private pilot's licence. Peter appeared kind and normal, and this time, after several long honest heart-felt conversations on the phone, we agreed to meet. This time I took the initiative and decided he would drive to meet me at a location of my choice and I chose Hever Castle in Kent, the childhood home of Ann Boleyn.

A place with beautiful formal gardens and grounds to sit in or stroll around. We got on well and although, not necessarily my usual type, he was interesting intelligent and upwardly mobile. We sat by the 38 acre lake, the brainchild of William Waldorf Astor, a tranquil location to sit and reflect, slightly away from the castle and gardens. The magical lakeside area of the Italian loggia and Japanese Tea house provided wonderful points to view the lake and had stunning vistas.

It was a romantic place indeed. Afterwards, we had lunch together at a nearby pub. It had been such a perfect day and we agreed to meet again.

On August bank holiday weekend, Peter invited me to Oxford for the weekend where I would meet and get to know one of his daughters and her family. Peter appeared to be a very formal person and a gentleman, and I was treated accordingly. I felt safe in his company and it was lovely meeting his daughter, her husband and 3 children. I was taken out for dinner in Oxford and invited to stay over in one of his guest rooms in his substantial home.

On his suggestion, we were to explore some of the lovely North Cotswolds villages the following day. Peter had planned the weekend beautifully and he was to drive me around in his Red Ferrari that he kept for high days and holidays.

I loved Oxford and it's cultural heritage and the surrounding countryside. It was so close to Gloucestershire which was a county I had close affiliations and a history with. Indeed, I had spent 4 years living in the village of Stanton near Broadway and so we agreed to go and pay a nostalgic visit back down memory lane.

I hadn't been back to Stanton since I had moved away from Gloucestershire and the memories from the time I had lived there had been traumatic and very painful. My son had died in a car crash and Paul, my husband, had gone through his bankruptcy, and our relationship had taken a turn for the worse during that time. On top of all that, we had become homeless while there.

I wondered whether it was a good idea to go back in case any memories triggered psychological trauma; indeed I was feeling very hesitant. Trauma is perhaps the most avoided, ignored, belittled, denied, misunderstood and untreated cause of human suffering. I had lived through it and had barely survived it. Still, I had spent years in self-taught therapy and healing, so perhaps it would be a test to see how far I'd come on my journey. So I bravely decided to test this hypothesis and see what happened next.

I had not been driven in a Ferrari before. Built for speed and not comfort, some models certainly tested your levels of comfort and endurance over long distances, and bumpy roads were definitely unforgiving. Originally, these cars were built for speed and power. I also learnt that in addition to most purchasers needing to prove they had owned Ferraris before, age was a factor as well, as many dealers wouldn't sell to someone under the age of 40.

Still, it was an exciting ride and we got noticed wherever we went. As we left Oxford, the thrill of the ride kicked in as the cabin vibrated with a sound that was high and animalistic, a ferocious creature scrabbling in the engine bay behind me, anxious to break free. Peter stepped on the gas, and holy gobsmack! My body was stuffed into the seat, my bones marrow cooked, and soft viscera muddled into jelly. This was unlike any car I had ever been in and gosh, it was terribly sexy.

As we passed the beautiful Oxfordshire countryside with its honeyed-coloured houses and green and pleasant lands, heading towards Gloucestershire, I relaxed and decided to immerse myself in the experience. Our first stop was at the famous Burford Garden Centre; a familiar place I had visited regularly when I had lived in the county.

Founded in 1975 by Nigel Johnson and his family, Burford Garden Company has grown into a one of a kind destination store for those seeking a unique, curated mixture of plants, gardenalia, home décor, furniture, art clothing and food to reflect their individual style.

The company drew inspiration from the very latest garden and interior trends, an ever-changing visual feast of handpicked and unique products. The 15 acre store was a very personal place to shop. From giant string lit orchid trees, kitchen tables that seated 16 people, the aroma of freshly baked cakes or romantic oversized Italian rose arbours, Burford Garden Centre was a feast for the eyes and soul. We had coffee and a wander around for an hour and then continued our journey towards the villages in and around Stow on the Wold.

I remembered it all so well and vowed that one day, I would return and buy my own little cottage somewhere close by. I had happy memories of my house on the Cotswolds Way with my daughter riding on her pony; happy times before all hell had broken loose.

Finally, we arrived in Stanton village in the civil parish of Tewkesbury and at the foot of the Cotswolds escarpment, about 2½ miles southwest of Broadway. It had access to the Cotswolds Way with good walking and riding, and with the village was built almost completely of Cotswold stone, a honeyed-coloured Jurassic limestone. Several of the cottages had thatched roofs and its high street and pub was all it contained. It was architecturally the most distinguished of the smaller villages in the North Cotswolds.

Peter pulled up outside Cross Cottage, a honey stone period grade II listed cottage and the dear little home I had once rented for 4 years with the medieval Cross monument situated outside. It was such a stunning and quintessential Cotswold village rural location. A gathering of horses and riders came down the high street, back from their ride on the Cotswolds Way, just like they had always done since the day I had moved into the cottage.

One of the riders commented jokingly on Peter's Ferrari and said with a smile how she was jealous that we had more horse power than herself. I looked at the cottage with affection and allowed myself to feel any flow of emotion and connection I had towards it, but weirdly, I felt nothing other than a tinge of sadness and the belief that I had to come back to realise that I had finally moved on in my life and my healing journey had made huge advances.

Believing very much in no such thing as coincidence, I knew the universe had chosen Peter to bring me back there for that reason. I believe that meeting people is never an accident. Someone cannot walk in and out of your life without reason. Lessons and the growth that you experience are never spontaneous. It is always meant to be. I believe that there is a higher purpose, an end beyond you and me, which we will never know until we reach it.

It helps you flourish and teaches you the important lessons that only people and their existence can give you. There IS a plan for us, and we must find it if we want to conquer it.

If you think about it, in a world that has 7.442 billion people, each capable of teaching you something, why did your path cross with that person? Because you needed a particular lesson at that point in your life. Think about it deeply, only then will you start treating your growth not as an accident but seeing it as a beautiful journey meant just for you.

The data of neuroscience shows us that we are not broken at all, and that our autonomic nervous system does not speak a verbal language. The language that our systems do understand is an embodied one; we have to show, not tell, our systems that we are safe now. This very old model of mental health has shown people that they are broken or suffer from dysfunction, but that's not true; that's not what science is telling us nowadays.

It's extraordinary how resilient and unbroken people are. We most certainly can heal, we most certainly can regulate, we are not stuck for decades, these things can get discharged and leave our bodies, and we can be free of them, I was an example of this, although it had taken many years to get there.

We proceeded to take a little walk around the beautiful village and then decided to head back to Oxford via the winding country lanes, finally arriving back at Peter's house several hours later. The drive had taken its toll. As I got out of the car, my body protested profusely with the aches and pains I had gained that day due to being driven around in a Ferrari. I decided that it had been the most uncomfortable drive of my life, and yet the most thrilling.

As I left Peter to drive the 3-hour journey back home to Tunbridge Wells, I thought it had been a lovely weekend and a necessary visit back to my past. Peter and I had one more meet-up several weeks later. I had driven down this time to Cheltenham to see my cousin and as Peter was close by in Oxford, it made sense to meet up.

Sadly, and with what seemed out of character for him, he stood me up for dinner that evening with the excuse that he had been delayed by a plumber coming to fix a leak at his home. We met for brunch the next day instead, but I decided then and there that this had been an excuse and that he had other stuff going on. I was intuitive and instantly knew a 'porky Pie' when I heard one.

He could have let me know beforehand rather than waiting for me to call him. I hadn't liked his rudeness and disrespect. I decided he was not the man for me. My tolerance nowadays was limited and picking up on derogatory sexist remarks he had casually made about women, which were admittedly jocular, and the change in his behaviour that weekend gave me concerns.

With a plethora of knowledge on unhealthy relationships and the ability to spot red flags when they arose, I was not prepared to settle for that kind of behaviour, so I ended it then and there.

I could now pick up on that kind of energy in a second. I am sure I was not the woman for him either. I suspect my belief system, ways of seeing things, and being my authentic self proved a challenge for him. He had mentioned that I was 'deep' and in some ways that had been a criticism and negative comment. I did not need validation from him.

Why does one ever need validation from another human being? Why do we not see ourselves as a loving, powerful, and valuable person? It denies one's divinity; it means you do not see yourself as a loving powerful person.

We got back in touch a year later as he was following me on Facebook and liked a couple of my posts. We had spoken on the phone and I had told him that his previous behaviour had shocked and surprised me. He admitted that he had regrets about his past behaviour and was sorry, confirming that his behaviour was also not received well by other women he had met.

He said, "Don't worry, Sara, it was not you. I have had similar reactions from other women." It was kind of him to be that honest and upfront without ego, so we agreed to remain friends going forward, and he was, in fact, incredibly helpful by agreeing to become a reference for my Ofsted enhanced DBS checking.

My short experience with the dating scene and these men had left me feeling disappointed and frustrated. Still, I acknowledged that I just hadn't found the right person yet, and finding an evolved person who was spiritually on the same level as me was going to take time.

A lot of the men around the age of 60 years old that I had engaged with had antiquated views of women and low levels of consciousness. They had not evolved in their thinking either and certainly did not have the emotional intelligence I wanted in a relationship.

I understood that not everyone has a spiritual side to them, and that some people don't understand the power of using our soul, and that we go from a physical power, or an emotional power, to the 'power of self' to eventually trusting to the power of God, or source energy, to working through our lives, which is a whole new journey.

When someone is so entrenched in the physical world, it's difficult for them to even conceive of trusting something in the airwaves, when anything of any value for them is what they can only touch, hear, see or smell.

Everyone deserves romantic love but not everyone qualifies to take part in it. Like qualifications when applying for a job, qualifications are necessary for being a romantic partner. Just because we are all worthy of love, it does not always mean we are able to give and receive it in ways that support it to thrive.

Being in a relationship requires intention, awareness, reflection, accountability, humility, courage, practice, and skilfulness, and letting go of your pride and ego. It is not always easy to make relationships work, and anyone who says otherwise is mistaken.

I was asking for my needs to be met this time and also for what I lacked in my childhood. We all have wounds from unmet needs in childhood that occur without explanation or empathy. I now believed in talking care of my inner child by prioritising those needs that still lived within me. Building trust with my inner child by using discernment to see who I chose was vitally important to me.

To deepen my self-respect and self-trust, I knew what the qualifications needed to be from someone I wanted to be with me. I also was aware that I needed to consider the qualifications I needed to be for someone too.

Qualities I was looking for were the ability to reflect on their patterns of behaviour, take accountability for their mistakes, and actively work on their growth. The ability to apologise with sincerity without spiralling into shame and blame. The healing of inter-generational trauma and rework of dysfunctional patterns. Someone who practices empathy and sensitivity to feelings and someone who lives in their body and is awake to the moment.

Emotionally mature in validating my experiences, even if different from their own. Honest in themselves about their boundaries and someone who shares transparency. The list was long and I was in no way unrealistic in finding such a person as I knew it would be a rare find indeed, but it was more about honouring myself this time and knowing what I needed and letting that influence who I deepened with.

Our standards in relationships are ours to claim and our dealbreakers are ours to know. Our core needs are the barometer for who to be with. The more you trust yourself to have your inner child's back, the more you choose to be with people who are trustable.

Having clear boundaries and direct communication revealing our truth, honouring our needs, making requests and owning what is ours helps us no longer have to use outdated strategies to stay safe in ways that worsen the dynamic and keep us from what we want. We must be willing to give up a part of ourselves and find a balance between who we are and who we want to be.

Of course, sacrifice is necessary at times, and no one is perfect, but by understanding and respecting one another, something special can be achieved.

Many of us want unconditional love and understanding, but we are not always willing to accept each other's flaws and imperfections. I was not looking for the perfect one, instead, I was looking for someone who complimented me and made me feel alive, someone who supported my dreams and who admired my strengths and also helped overcome my weaknesses.

Someone who understood what it is like to be under pressure and has the courage to face their own demons while helping me face mine. In the end, what matters most I guess is finding someone who made me happy, everything else is secondary. It's ok to be alone but not completely. Someone to lean on and to be able to talk with without fear or judgement is key.

In November of 2021, feeling slightly deflated given the emotional being that I am, I started feeling lonely and a little despondent and missing my son, Daniel, my parents my brother and loved ones who were now deceased. Missing the security of a loving family home and the connection to all of that. With abandonment issues rising to the forefront and depression and sadness starting to engulf me, I allowed old patterns of negative thinking to creep back in.

I knew that I had abandonment issues from losing so many of my loved ones, and I was I working very hard to heal my suffering, but the mind loves repetition and if you are not constantly mindful, old patterns of thinking and cognitive distortions can sneak back into our psyches.

While going about my everyday business at work out shopping one day, I went into a lighting shop in Tunbridge Wells with one of my blonde curly-haired cherub looking children and striking up a conversation with its owner, who happened to mention that the child with me looked like his own son when he had been little, telling me that he died in his 30s of cancer.

We had an interesting conversation about faith and the possibility of life after death. I told him that my own daughter, April, had sort a psychic medium to contact her own grandmother and I had told him the story of what had happened and how it had led to the meeting with her psychic.

I told him he could contact his son any time he liked and he proceeded to tell me his own mother also had dealings with such things. My daughter frequently said she had seen my mother, an apparition of a red-headed lady in our old home, The Rectory, throughout her childhood. She had even been in a new age crystal shop when the owner told her that her grandmother was trying to make contact with her and he promptly gave her a personal message from her.

The lighting shop owner had asked me if I knew of a psychic medium and if I could help him contact his son. I did not know of anyone at that point in time and leaving the shop, I continued to go about my everyday business knowing that there is no such thing as a coincidence and that in some ways, I had meant to go into his shop to help him for a reason.

A couple of weeks later, I had driven out to a local East Sussex village to a haberdashery shop looking for vintage buttons for an old coat of mine, when the lady in the shop started talking openly and friendly. She was an artist and was temporarily helping out in the shop for a friend whose husband had sadly recently died of cancer.

Low and behold, after half an hour of chatting, she mentioned a friend of hers who was a psychic medium! I hadn't told her my story of meeting the lighting shop owner or anything along the lines of the subject of the afterlife. I knew instantly this was meant for me. What are the odds that a conversation like that should have occurred!

It never ceases to amaze me 'the powers that be' and that nothing is a coincidence. Leaving without my vintage buttons, instead of with the contact details of a psychic medium, I proceeded to go to the gentleman in the lighting shop, giving him the psychic medium's details. It was a Friday morning and he was delighted by my gift and proceeded to tell me it was his best day ever.

I believe we are sometimes used to doing the angel's work for them, and it made me so happy to be able to make a difference for good in someone else's life. I now had the opportunity to make contact with my own dearly beloved departed relatives and I contacted the psychic medium straight away for my own appointment.

On 6 of November 2021, I found myself arriving outside a pretty white weather-boarded Kent cottage dating back to the 17th century on the outskirts of Tunbridge Wells. As I walked up the garden path, bordered by manicured box hedging and a rose-covered arbour, I was delighted at the surroundings I found myself in as David, the psychic medium, greeted me at the door.

Once inside, it's impressive exposed walls and ceiling beams gave a historical nod to its architectural heritage and enormous charm. It really was a beautiful home and tastefully decorated with furniture suiting its history. I did not know what to expect as I was invited into his sitting room, but I was made to feel very welcome as I was asked to sit down on the chair provided.

David was kind and easy to be around, aged around 60 and very handsome, he told me that he had inherited the psychic gift from his mother as far back as the age of 8 years old. We were to record the session on my mobile phone so I could listen to it after I went home and make sense of anything later on that I fully didn't understand during the time spent with David that afternoon.

I was asked to relax, put my feet firmly on the ground and do a little exercise to ground myself a little more. I took three deep breaths in and held them for a few seconds releasing slowly. As I was taking the breath in, I was to think of taking in positive energy and when releasing the breath, I was to think of blowing out any negative energy. This was to ground me and prepare me to take on board whatever came through.

David did the same and then we waited to see what happened. I was told that sometimes the messages are not necessarily for me, they could be for anyone in the family and might not necessarily make sense to me, hence the recording of it to share with other family members or friends at a later time. I was told the spirit world may have family that wouldn't do this sort of thing, and therefore, I may be used to getting messages through to another family or persons.

If anything didn't make sense, I was to say so because it meant David wouldn't go down the wrong track and if it did make sense, I was to say yes as this would make the energy go up, and he would get freezing cold and then he will know he had got a connection. He said I should feel it as well.

The first thing David picked up on was seeing a red tractor in the distance and a ploughed field. He said it's just there not doing anything but it felt just out in the countryside. There was a connection to me and the countryside or I was brought up there. It was a very still and calm place, peaceful and that I knew that when I went there. They showed him a 'wiggle road' or path, I'd had lots of 'twists and turns', and told him that I looked very calm and collected now as I sat in front of David, but I had had a lot of trauma in my life.

They said I was starting to get back on track but had come off track quite a bit. They said she isn't who she really is; she is very good at putting up a screen to cover her feelings, and they said they were not putting me down. They just said we know what I've been through. They showed David a broken heart and he got instantly emotional and had to stop himself from crying as the feeling engulfed him.

He was told by them that I was tough and that I didn't think I was, and that whatever had happened to me had made me strong and that I had come back stronger than I ever was before. David also said that there was an event, anniversary or birthday or something important I had forgotten.

The spirit world did not tell him what I had gone through in my past, only that I had to go through what I had for some reason. David saw himself standing on a cliff wanting to throw himself off. David asked me if I had ever felt like that, to which I replied yes. Everything he had said so far was absolutely correct. He sensed desperation but knew I'd had much more to live for.

He told me that no one who ever knew me knew this was going on because I didn't open up to many people. He then saw a railway track and said he sometimes gets mixed up with just tracks. He asked the word 'help' and the spirit world turned the tracks up to produce a ladder, depicting an uphill climb. I got so far up and then came back down again, but I would not give in. I would fight whatever it was I was dealing with; again they did not tell him what it was.

He was seeing my digestive system and intestines and asked if I had problems there or within that area. Later on in the session, I was told that my heart, instinct and everything I feel, is in this area. Then suddenly, someone came in; it was my grandmother on my paternal side. David said she felt really tiny and slightly stooped. She blended in a little bit but wasn't telling him who she was or a name.

The letter M appeared (maybe mother) but it could mean anything. They picked up on my reiki connection. David was seeing a sound bowl and they were telling David that they were very proud of me. I had been through untold Hell to get where I am now and I had to do it as there was no choice. I had reached a point where I had to do whatever I had to do. So now I felt free but wished I hadn't had to go through what I had to get there.

Twenty minutes into the 2-hour session, my father came in to give me a hug. I was told that we were very close to each other. He said that if he had been here at the time, he would have helped me. He said he'd been trying to help in other ways. Part of why I was seeing David was down to him because he didn't know any way else of helping me. He apologised that it had taken so long but he said I wasn't ready for it then.

David said my father looked very smart and very dapper. My father told David that he believed in free speech; he believed in saying what you really felt, obviously without hurting people's feelings. He had felt slightly trapped in what he did as well. He did what he did to earn money but it wasn't really him. So he said in the time he was born, you just had to do whatever came along, and if you had a bit of an inkling for something, you went for it or you did what your father did and you were pushed.

My father said if he had his time again, he wouldn't do career-wise what he did. He said he understood where I was coming from now because I was just beginning to find out who I really was and it was a revelation and it's great. He said he applauds me for what I've done and for what I've been through. David said he thought it was his mother with him because they were together and again mentioned that she was so tiny.

My grandmother had died before I was born so I couldn't confirm what she had looked like. David told me she was not simple, but uncomplicated and happy with her own lot. She just liked looking after the family and doing whatever it was she needed to do. She told David, and he laughed, that she didn't believe in all that women's lib stuff. She had enjoyed her life and she had been happy.

She said she understood if people are in a situation where they are not happy and need to move on. She understood what I'd done, but she was happy with what happened to her in her lifetime. She wasn't judging me; if she had been in the same boat as me, she would have done the same thing.

My father, whose name was Geoffrey, had been a strikingly handsome and fashionable man, 6 ft tall and slim with blonde hair; a highly sensitive and reactive man, and somewhat vain. He was known to stand in front of the mirror and comb his hair for hours on end while contemplating life. He slept walked as a child and his parents had sort medical attention for this.

Complex, kind and generous from an East End of London background with a history of ancestors born into poverty and the workhouse. His ancestors had scrambled to raise themselves up out of poverty and he had become successful through sheer hard graft. When alive, he regarded himself as different from the average person, sometimes referring to them as 'joe bloggs' or 'the great unwashed', therefore elevating himself within society and making him judgemental and rather a snob.

This attitude was drummed into us children from very early age, giving us unrealistic attitude towards people and life. As he advanced through life and became successful, his newspaper of choice was *The Daily Telegraph* which showed he saw himself as elitist and signified he had now arrived amongst the middle classes.

Like many people from poorer backgrounds, he could not handle stress very well and had externalising coping mechanism problems which resulted too often in him yelling, fighting, refusal to comply and sometimes aggressive behaviour. He also had a strong need to control others and he was at times highly unstable. He had fully come into himself and wanted to exceed his own expectations, therefore he worked extremely hard and pushed himself to provide for his family with a comfortable lifestyle.

Image was important to him too. In his lifetime, he had travelled to lovely places and owned beautiful houses and drove nice cars, dressed nicely and ate in decent restaurants. A rather insular man, his family was everything to him. A dedicated family man who adored his daughter and she adored him in return. Unable to show love demonstratively, he would buy things to show his love and affection, and consequently, as a family, we wanted for nothing.

He had married my mother who was a beautiful woman and above his social station coming from old family money, yet at times he became frustrated with his wife's comfortable middle class attitude. He suffered anxiety and sometimes depression and he only chose a few friends who could advance his expectations and position. Coming from a lower-quality environment had caused him to have strained relations with his own parents.

He found life hard and when it challenged him in the 1980s recessions, causing him to lose his business and all his material wealth, he reacted by drinking alcohol in large quantities to be able to cope, and this was what killed him at the age of 50 years old.

David picked up on the fact that my father died alone and that it didn't matter. My father said it was easier to pass when someone wasn't there as the love keeps us here and makes it harder to leave. Apparently, a deceased hearing is the last to go and although dead, they can still hear for a bit and get frustrated because they want to say something when family are around them saying goodbye. Dad wanted me to know this because he knew it troubled me that I was not with him when he died and to let go of that feeling.

Thirty minutes into my time with David, he started to get a clearer picture of what had happened to me in my life and started to relay and confirm situations and of course, yet again, he was absolutely correct. He confirmed that my husband was delusional. Of course, he could have been referring to my first husband, Chris, who had abandoned me and his three children while they were growing up.

It could have also been my second husband, Paul. He said to this day, he did not believe he had done anything wrong in his past demeanours, 'what's all the fuss about' and 'she's going crackers' and making it all up. David said that was the feeling he was getting.

He said my second husband, Paul, had the ability to twist people around his little finger. He's very clever at taking people in, and that was why it was so difficult for me to prove what he had been doing and what I'd had gone through. I was told categorically not to get sucked back in again because, at one point, I thought of going back. Why go through all this because' better the devil you know'?

David said my relatives in the spirit world don't want me to go back with him. They can only advise but not tell me what to do. Deep down, I knew and understood that you cannot have a happy ending to a journey that has not been pleasant along the way. The end absolutely does not justify the means. The means, or the path along the way, always brings about the essence of an identical ending.

David then proceeded to talk about me starting a women's/ men's support group or getting in touch with people who had gone through the same thing or were in the same boat as myself. He said my experiences could help other women. I then told him that I had written a book about my experiences specifically to help those such people. I didn't feel that David was 'cold reading' me like some sceptics might imagine, it felt totally authentic.

At that moment, and with such clarity, I knew this was my 'calling' and that everything I had experienced this far in my life had led me to this moment. He told me that I spent years saying sorry yet I've done nothing wrong. And then, the awful thing that had haunted me through all of this trauma and the thing I was never able to fully come to terms with and escape surfaced.

He apologised before he said it and said, "I don't know why I'm hearing this but I've got to say it," and then those immortal words left his mouth. "I'm sorry but I have to say the word prostitute."

My heart naturally skipped a beat. He apologised again but then proceeded to tell me that my husband had made me feel totally worthless on top of everything else. He encouraged me to write more books and then got an image of me on a TV program and radio station. David mentioned he heard the word 'self-worth', and when I look at myself in the mirror, I don't see who I truly am. I only see a shattered and broken person and I don't like who I am.

He said that's not because you don't really like who you are, it's how you've become through your suffering and what you've been through; body image stuff. It was going to take time to love myself again.

Spring time was my time of emergence David said and he got Easter as the time when I fully emerged into myself and who I really am with time on my own, where I looked after just me. Time on my own with space and time to be quiet whereby I was not reliant on any man, finding time on my own whereby I had found peace and security which was all down to me.

I had worked hard for all of that and I must not get drawn back into any of that stuff again. The spirit world said you don't need David to tell you what you need to do, just go with your gut instinct, which you've already done. Embrace who you are, your motives are good, and have faith in yourself as you are a good person. He confirmed my affinity with nature and how I suck up all the energy and how it rejuvenates me when I'm among it.

Things were moving forward for me because finally, I believed in who I am. He said it's when we don't believe in ourselves that we can't move forward.

Listening to David repeat all these messages in exactly the vocabulary and diction my relatives would have used, confirmed it was actually them speaking to us. His analysis of my life and the troubles I had incurred in my life journey thus far were spot-on and accurate. It gave me huge comfort to be with him and finally be understood by someone. I felt my family were still around watching and listening to me and any feelings of abandonment and being left behind vanished, knowing I was surrounded by them always in spirit.

David briefly referred to the village I had been in where I had met his friend, Cindy, in the haberdashery shop that had led me to him, and made the link to the church and Rectory where I had once lived and how I was disillusioned by religion. We had a brief interlude where he told me that he wasn't a spiritualist despite there being a spiritual union and that he refused to belong to it.

As the session continued well into the next hour, I was to hear from my son, Daniel, as he came through the medium and all my hopes for this connection were honoured.

We all come into this world with what David called a bucket list. We have all had lives before, we've all done different things and we've all had to learn different things in different lives. Some people ask why we have had to go through the things we have. Sometimes you breeze through one life, you have a break, and in another life, you'll have lots of ups and downs and ask 'why me?'

David said, "Why not you?" We've all had illnesses and all sorts of things happen to us, but usually, when we look back at what's happened to us, we've become a stronger person because of it. None of us like what we've had to go through. You just have to be who you are and be true to yourself. We can't always be friends with everyone or get on with everyone. Sometimes people come into our lives for a long time and some for a short period of time.

You can connect with a person, but when they have given you what you need, they have to move on. You take from them what you need, again you give out energy to other people, and you move on. In a way, it's lovely because everyone is helping everyone; we are all connected. Sometimes we don't like who we connect with but we can't judge because we don't know what they are going through.

David took hold of my hands to make a stronger connection and felt a tingling sensation and asked if there was a connection to Italy and Spain and said he could almost see me living out there as the way of life suited me better as I don't like the madness of a town or city. Maybe once a year for six months to recharge and rejuvenate and to write more books.

Also, that I have opened up a portal or avenue of unlocked expression within me because I hadn't been able to express myself fully in the past. To do this, I needed to be somewhere quiet and peaceful. He said it's allowing myself permission to be truly me. He then asked me if I had 3 children, I told him that I had 4, and he confirmed 3 girls and felt that the other child had not been here long.

Then Daniel, my son, came and spoke through David. He said, "The reason I left was because you gave me the love I needed. I never had love like I had with you." So he said my purpose in life was to feel what it was like to feel love because he had previous lives where he never felt loved. He didn't need to have a whole lifetime David said, and what I gave him was what he came here for.

So my darling son said it was not a bad thing, but a good thing. Whatever I did or didn't do, he would have gone anyway. So he said don't be sad, because I gave him what he needed.

Daniel told the medium that I carry around something of his. David said I don't know what it is. Then I showed him the tattoo of Daniel's name imprinted on my left inside wrist. Again, my son said, "Don't be sad, I'm fine. I watch over you all the time, I'm growing all the time." He said he was very grateful for being a part of my life. He told David that I had definitely felt him, whether it was in a dream or a smell.

He said I've come to you and you were not sure if it was true, but he said you know that it was so vivid, it wasn't a normal dream, it didn't vanish and it's still with you. Daniel confirmed that I was not going crackers. I came when you needed it. He said I've got an old man's head on my shoulders now. He came in as an old soul and had learnt so much in the short time I was with you.

David said my son's name at this point. He wants you to let go of the guilt of his passing. He said, "Don't feel guilty, Mum. No need to feel guilty. I came into this world knowing what I needed to do and what I wanted." He said, "I'm sorry if what I selfishly wanted to disrupt your life, but you have become stronger through that." David told me there had been an accident, and Daniel said that he was not disfigured.

He looked like he was asleep. "At least you have that memory of me and that I am whole now anyway. I just happened to be in the wrong place at perhaps the right time."

I was told that when a certain sound comes on the radio while I am driving and I think it's connected to Daniel, I am not going mad, it is Daniel trying to connect with me and letting me know he is around and trying to help me. He does this and it's not a coincidence. He said "I am growing up and I'm learning. I'm just cherishing every moment that I had with the whole family."

But, he said some of us die younger than others. "Don't forget that's just a body, the soul inside is always; it never dies. So I haven't died, I haven't gone anywhere."

I then asked David, "Where is he then?" David replied he's just not in that body anymore, he's just doing what he needs to do. There are plains, he said it would blow your mind if I tried to explain because we are not meant to know really; it is too complicated to explain.

Daniel mentioned that his funeral was packed and that a letter was put in his coffin. He wanted me to know that he didn't feel anything, it was really quick. "One minute I was there, then the next I was gone. I just popped out of my body." He said, "I didn't feel it. Don't have regrets, Mum. Don't have guilt because you couldn't do anymore; it's just the way it was. Try and get rid of that thought, you have enough on your plate, you don't need to carry that around with you."

Again he confirmed it was his time and that we would meet again sometime, but he said I had lots and lots to do first.

David then said that this didn't help my relationship with my husband and that it almost finished the relationship as I didn't get the support I needed. My husband shut down and we couldn't talk to each other. I needed to talk, so he has a lot of issues and needs to speak to someone. David knew that my son was obsessed with cars, and then David repeated what my son said.

"I was inexperienced. I wasn't an experienced driver. I thought I was, but I wasn't. I liked speed and if anyone is to blame, it's me." David laughed and said he had a good sense of humour as he said, "What a way to go!" Again, Daniel told David that I had forgotten something, a date, anniversary, birthday, but at this point, I still could not remember what that was. David was seeing the number 7 and didn't know why.

I told him I had 7 children including my stepchildren. He told me that was another issue. They don't always get on and there were resentments there.

Later on a couple of weeks later, I remembered that I had forgotten Daniel's daughter's birthday and that she had just turned 7 years old. Daniel's daughter, Francesca, my granddaughter, had been born two months after his accident. Her mother had not been able to cope hence she had been adopted. I was told Daniel was 'jack the lad' and lit the room up, a cheeky chappy with a heart of gold. He did naughty tricks on people but was harmless.

He would do anything for anybody. He said, "I am with you every step of the way, Mum." His love of music was mentioned, especially his eclectic tastes and he approved of the music played at his funeral. "They did a good job," he said. "I want you to know I was really pleased with what we did." Joking, Daniel then showed David a coffin on the side of a motorbike. "He thinks that would have been great!"

He wanted to give his love to everybody and let them know he comes to everybody when he can. "I try and help everybody as much as I can, but at the moment, I'm trying to cope with my new life. I'm learning to do what I need to do here. It does not mean I've gone completely but it's becoming less and less of me coming in, but I need you to know I am around."

He then shows David the farm connection where he lived with us for a while and tells David it was idyllic. "I couldn't have been happier. I'm so grateful for what I have, don't think of me in the past but the present, because that person you still love is here. I just don't have the earthly body. My spirit lives on, we never die."

Then David said he wants to give you a hug and just like Oda Mae Brown (whoopee Goldberg) in the film *Ghost*, David got up and gave me a huge hug with Daniel inside of him. Then he said, "Love you, Mum."

Chapter 3

Christmas 2021 came and went with Boris Johnson giving the country the go-ahead without any curbs on socialising, prompting warnings that this could lead to tougher measures later despite tentative signs that cases of the virus had begun to plateau. The prime minister said he understood that families across England needed certainty to press ahead with Christmas plans but warned curbs could still be imposed after 25 December because of the rapid spread of the Omicron variant.

After having spent a quiet one with just Paul, my daughter, Summer, and myself here in Tunbridge Wells in my rented cosy little flat, hunkering down while a new wave of the Omicron variant of the Corona Virus hit the UK, the New Year was welcomed in with the Hypergraphia to write. Many of us carry stories inside us that need releasing and it's important to do so while the fire is still inside of us. My need to write about my life and how I dug myself out of the darkness using writing as my crutch and what I had learnt from it was becoming my passion.

Some say that writing isn't suited to an extroverted nature; it can be too solitary, too slow and too boring, but I found it to be exciting and liberating. There is a great quote by Henry

David Thoreau which says 'Write while the heat is in you. The writer who postpones the recording of his thoughts uses an iron which has cooled to burn a hole with. He cannot inflame the minds of his audience'.

I was discovering the healing powers of writing as I came to terms with my grief and writing was becoming my lifesaver. I wanted 2022 to be a game changer year. My first book was to be published this year and as the excitement was building I was feeling joy and exhilaration mixed with feelings of frustration as I wanted it to happen quickly, instead of having to wait until November when the book signing and media coverage was to start. Still, it was really happening and I was feeling ecstatic.

The reality though was that bills and rent still needed paying and so I had to work my childcare jobs until I found another source of income.

My subscription to the dating website was coming to an end and with only two possible matches in six months, I decided not to renew it. These things were costly and my commitment to contributing a financial fee to my publisher was more important. Literally a couple of days before it ran out, I was contacted by a gentleman, this time in my hometown of Tunbridge Wells.

After a couple of phone calls and me googling the web to check and do my due diligence, we agreed to meet for a coffee in a local hotel close by. On meeting this very pleasant man, I was to discover that he was a healthcare practitioner working in Chinese medicine and acupuncture with his own clinic in Bromley.

I had met a similar individual to myself who understood holistic medicine, energy work, and the healing of the mind body and spirit; this was a rare find indeed. Clearly, he had been very successful in his field and had made a name for himself specialising in treating fertility problems in women and skin conditions. His work had taken him all over the world and at one time, he had three clinics in the London area.

He had studied in China, learning his profession from the masters and had actually studied it in Mandarin. I discovered he had lied on his dating profile stating he was age 58 when he was actually 10 years older than that, but he did own up immediately saying no one would have looked at him on the app otherwise and he certainly didn't look his age.

It soon became clear that we had so much in common and connected on so many levels which I found just wonderful. He definitely was a fascinating and interesting individual to talk to and that first date lasted 2½ hours.

We agreed to another date, this time going out for dinner in a local Turkish restaurant. I was to discover, like myself, he hated exploitation, unfair treatment and human suffering. He told me that had recently been in a high court case in London whereby he had taken to court a farmer and land owner neighbour who had tried to swindle him and his neighbours out of land and boundaries he had previously sold them.

The farmer in question had apparently been an evil individual poisoning animals and manipulating people with threats to get his own way.

It had been an unpleasant court case whereby the farmer had lied in court and had even tried to manipulate the judge with fake illnesses to stall court proceedings. All of this my new friend, Terry, had counteracted upon by secretly filming the farmer when he was supposed to be visiting a hospital but was found to be elsewhere, determined not to allow the farmer to get away with anything.

It had taken three years to conclude the case and had dominated and consumed his life, costing him half a million pounds in legal fees in the process.

The story had made the national newspaper and eventually, my friend won his case but the proceedings had left him hugely depleted in the pocket and psychologically affected, whereby he could not stay in his beautiful home because it now had unpleasant associations attached to it. But he had won and had stopped the bully from wreaking havoc on people's lives.

He finally had the justice he set out to get. The farmer in question having lost the case and his name as well as all of his money he used to fight it, had committed suicide by hanging himself. Shortly after this, the farmer's son had done the same. What a tragic ending and concludes 'the sins of the father'.

These individuals who stand up to bullies are rare and courageous beings indeed. It takes huge conviction to stand up and fight for what is morally right. I hardly knew this man, we'd only just met, but I already loved him for this and was determined to become his friend. When we stand up for our rights, and what we believe in, there is always a chance we risk the very thing we fight for, our safety, our lives, our freedom. But if we stand down, the risk is definite.

Strong people stand up for themselves, but stronger people stand up for others and because of this, these people are rare. Sadly though, I did not fancy him or have that romantic spark, so we agreed to become just friends.

Soon afterwards, I was to discover from my middle daughter, April, that her grandmother, aged 92, died peacefully in her sleep. She had complained of feeling dizzy and while surrounded by her 3 sons visiting her that weekend in her home, she had taken to her bed for a few hours rest and had later died. My first husband and her eldest son had gone in to check on her and found her.

My daughter was clearly distressed and so I supported her the best way I could, but it had been difficult because I had disliked my mother-in-law from my first marriage intensely.

The family had affectionately nicknamed her 'The Bird' because she had been overly protective of her 3 sons and didn't really allow them to fully leave her nest. She had cosseted and smothered them all throughout their lives, Indeed her youngest son, aged 60, still lived at home with her.

I remember vividly her phoning pretty much every day when I had been married to her son, and even when we had been having carnal knowledge of one another, she would phone and interrupt us and my husband would always answer the call.

I blamed her for many of our marriage difficulties; there was definitely an Oedipus complex going on. She was prone to being rude and pushy, dominating and controlling and I felt that there had always been three people in our marriage. When we started having children, she tried to overly get involved, especially with the girls as she had always wanted a daughter of her own. She spoilt them rotten and, using her money and social status, she had given them everything they wanted and desired in life.

Also, she had pushed my own mother out of the picture, constantly talking and promoting her family line above ours and ignoring our existence. She hadn't had to work a day in her life outside of the home and, fortunately for her, her husband's banking career had left her not wanting for anything and with lots of time on her hands.

When we had divorced and I was with my second husband, she had even tried to push her way into our new lives and tried to have full access to the children. In most cases, this would have been a reasonable healthy situation for a grandmother to see her grandchildren, normally this would happen through contact with her son's access to his children, but her son was nowhere to be seen and had no consistent contact with his children.

She would undermine everything I did and try to usurp me and dominate, while interfering and suffocating us. It was as if the children belonged to her and her son's lineage and that she must have them at any cost, but the reality was that her son had abandoned his small children financially and emotionally and was living and working abroad. It was my new husband and I who had picked up the pieces and was fully raising them.

When the children were older and independent of me, she had seen an opportunity and swoon in, and took over my place. Also her son, their father, suddenly started embracing a relationship with his children now that they were older and adults. The reality was that now my new husband and I had done all the hard work of raising them, they had come in and had taken all the rewards and credit of our hard work.

Her spoiling had caused my eldest daughter especially to become entitled and demanding, and this caused difficult relations between her and I. Still, my children would not have a bad word said against her. They couldn't see any of this going on, naturally, they enjoyed all the love, attention and money from her and were somewhat brainwashed as always by her stories of the importance of her family lineage, and that they were a privileged part of it; except for my son who could see how she truly was.

While going through one of his difficult periods, he had gone to her for help and a place to stay, but she had thrown him out, leaving him homeless. She hadn't liked his behaviour and emotional outbursts, and she was incapable of understanding or acknowledging the damage his father had inflicted upon him emotionally in childhood which had caused these reactions.

She lived in a wealthy area of Sandbanks, Poole in Dorset, one of the most expensive addresses in the UK known as millionaires row and had financial security to help him. Her husband, now dead, left her financially strong and secure. She had spent years trying to gain complete access to her grandchildren and here she was now with the opportunity to help him, yet she had disregarded him.

It was like telling someone, I want you, you belong to us, be a part of this wonderful family and then when you submit to it, you are told you're not wanted, and that I won't help you. How does one emotionally process that?

Later on, my son had also gone to stay with his father in Cornwall where he ran a guest house with his new wife. He locked himself in one of the guest bedrooms he was staying in because he was depressed and withdrawn. His father screamed and shouted at him to come out and when he refused, his father kicked down the bedroom door. My first husband had a nasty temper, and lacked patience and understanding, therefore my son would not or could not live with him.

This rejection on top of his father's inability to nurture him and be a consistent figure in his life as a child had caused my son great mental torture. When my first husband abandoned his children, leaving me to raise them alone, abandonment had been a contributing factor to my son's problems and later demise. It had been emotional cruelty he had inflicted on him.

My mother-in-law's middle son had divorced his wife and had become unstable and abandoned his 4 children as well. He told his mother not to have anything to do with them (her grandchildren), otherwise he would disown her, of which she had agreed to. Secretly though, she had remote contact with them. With the youngest daughter, she helped her by letting her come to her house weekly to clean for her, but she wasn't allowed to spend time with them in their home or spend Christmas holidays and high days.

Now grown-up adults, these 4 individuals have huge trauma symptoms from being abandoned and rejected by their father and losing proper contact with their grandmother.

Despite my first husband's family social status and outwardly appearance as an upwardly mobile, respectable banking family, their inner workings were dysfunctional. In my opinion, they were delusional and would not accept criticism or fault, or take any accountability for their actions. Spiritual life requires forgiveness but with this one I struggled hugely. As an HSP, my own survival strategy enables me to be hugely observant.

After my son's accident and at his funeral wake, she criticised my step-son for getting drunk afterwards at a family gathering while dealing with his grief at the loss of his brother. She was incapable of processing any compassion or empathy. To my amazement, my first husband got really cross with her and confronted her, calling her a stupid old woman.

She was a controlling, dangerous and manipulative individual and I had disliked her and had huge issues with her. While her own funeral proceedings were taking place, I resolved myself to stay firmly away from any family politics and any involvement, and I was relieved that she had finally departed.

Being delusional, I was later to discover, meant being characterised by or holding idiosyncratic beliefs or impressions that are contradicted by reality or rational argument, typically as a symptom of a mental disorder. It was linked to schizophrenia and delusional paranoia, faulty judgement, and being mistaken often being a symptom. My first husband's family had a history of schizophrenia in their gene pool.

The youngest son had been on strong medication all of his life having been diagnosed with severe symptoms of the illness when it had come to light in his early 20s. He had even been given the barbaric electrical shock treatment. One of their great aunts who had lived in Jersey in the Channel Islands had it too, and I was told that it was genetic and could skip a generation in families.

My mother-in-law had been taken in and raised by her two aunts as a child. Her own parents had a farm in Jersey and while busy with 3 sons and the farm, her being the only daughter, she had been allowed to be raised with the comforts of living in the big farmhouse with her financially comfortable spinster aunts. While there, she had been given all the sophisticated benefits bequeathed by them and had led a completely different life from her farm worker parents and brothers.

Living with a schizophrenic aunt in the 1930s, she would have been subjected to its symptoms and social prejudices and the shame that came with the illness at that time. This must have had a huge impact on her life growing up.

People who were mentally unstable were met with extreme prejudice in these times and were immediately deemed irrelevant. They would have been looked down on in society for doing no harm but simply for being born the way they were. They were treated in the worst environments such as asylums and hospitals, and they were classed as a burden to society.

Schizophrenia is a long-term disorder of a type, involving a breakdown in the relation between thought, emotion, and behaviour, leading to faulty perception, inappropriate actions and feelings, withdrawal from reality and personal relationships into fantasy and delusions, and absence of mental fragmentation. The exact causes of schizophrenia are unknown.

Research suggests a combination of physical, genetic, psychological, and environmental factors can make a person more likely to develop the condition. Some people may be prone to it and a stressful or emotional life event might trigger a psychotic episode.

The lobotomy was performed widely from the 1930s to the 1940s to treat schizophrenia, severe anxiety, and depression. Also, hydrotherapy, metrazol convulsions, and insulin shock therapy; these methods gave way to psychotherapy in the 1940s but sadly, it is an incurable condition.

My mother-in-law's youngest son was very ill with the illness and was heavily medicated and lived alternating in care home facilities and with her in their home in Sandbanks Poole Dorset. There were many incidents whereby he had to be arrested or removed from society for improper behaviour and for causing social unrest.

My mother-in-law lived in a very smart communal block of apartments and had the humiliation of being told by the residential management of the block that either her son would have to be sectioned and removed or she would have to vacate the premises because of the disruption he continually caused her neighbours there.

Care in the community, also called Community Care, is a British policy of deinstitutionalisation, treating and caring for physically and mentally disabled people in their homes rather than in an institution. Institutional care was the target of widespread criticism during the 1960s and 1970s, but it was not until 1983 that Margaret Thatcher adopted a new policy of care after the Audit Commission published a report called 'Making a Reality of Community Care', which outlined the advantages of domiciliary care.

Although, this policy had been attributed to the then Margaret Thatcher government, community care was not a new idea. It had been around since the 1950s and its aim was a more cost effective way of helping people with mental health problems and physical disabilities by removing them from impersonal, often Victorian institutions, and caring for them in their own homes.

The reality for my parents-in-law was very difficult. Looking after someone with schizophrenia who was an adult and wanted the freedom to wander and mix socially was a huge burden and worry for them. How do you control a full-grown man when you start to get old and physically impaired?

A series of scandals in mental hospitals in the past had hit the headlines of newspapers telling stories of abuse and inhumane treatment of patients who were out of sight and out of mind of the public. Books had been published which exposed the poor quality of care within certain institutions, and in 1981, ITV did a documentary called *Silent Minority* which spotlighted the conditions of mental patients at the Boro Court Hospital in Caterham Surrey and brought issues to the public eye.

In the 1980s, there was increasing criticism and concern about the quality of long-term care for dependant people. There was also concern about experiences of people leaving long-term institutional care and being left to fend for themselves in the community, yet the government at the time was committed to the idea of care in the community. My parents-in-law were smack bang in the middle of all this caring for a very sick son.

When I met my first husband and fell in love with him at the tender age of 18, I hadn't thought to do research into the illness and the consequences of getting involved with a family who carried this disease. I was young, naïve, in love, and ignorant in its knowledge. I had made uninformed choices at that time, which now when I look back on, I regret. I can now see many of my negative and unhappy past experiences in my first marriage could have been avoided.

I feel rather shocked and stupid at the realisation of this, how different my experiences and life for myself would have been if I knew then what I know now, or if someone had told me the dangers of taking the route I did marry into a family with schizophrenia. Certainly, if I had known then what I know now about the illness, I would not have entered into a relationship with my husband and certainly not had children with him.

The severity of my mother-in-law's son's illness was a huge burden to her. At times, I had even heard her say that she 'wished that he was dead'. Shocking as that may sound, living and looking after someone with a chronic disorder is extremely difficult. Schizophrenia, as a severe mental disorder, made him have a hard time telling the difference between what was real and not real.

He couldn't keep a job or care for himself, including his personal hygiene. He would get involved with people in his local community and make a nuisance of himself. In his 30s, he had befriended a wealthy single woman who was a neighbour and had become obsessed and infatuated with her friendship.

She had a young daughter and her divorce had left her a financially comfortable individual in her own right. She had chosen to work from home as a therapeutic massage therapist. She thought she could heal my brother-in-law through alternative therapy and their friendship was responsible for taking him off his medication. Overtime, my parents-in-law were to discover her line of work had her entertaining men on her premises and the massage therapies were of sexual nature.

After a couple of years, there was a huge scandal whereby she was found dead in her home. She had been murdered by one of her clients and my mother-in-law's son, because of his illness, naturally had become a suspect.

I had been on holiday at the time with my second husband in Spain and while reading the UK papers, I came across her picture and the article. I had met her briefly years previously. She was a pretty tiny blonde woman, childlike and with a squeaky infantile voice. She had been dressed in designer clothing, handbags and shoes. The details of the murder had been shocking and she had been killed with a knife.

She tried to escape her attacker and locked herself in a bathroom and bled to death. Her daughter who had been away that weekend had found her days later. My mother-in-law's son had a hard time coming to terms with this loss and although, completely innocent of any involvement, became withdrawn as his illness made his grief and mourning especially difficult, and he was at times suicidal.

With him being a suspect, the whole investigation process had been extremely unpleasant and embarrassing for the family.

My choice of partner in my first marriage had made my life impossibly problematic and difficult over the years and all the situations I had faced with this husband and his family were caused by elements of this debilitating illness. It permeated their inner world and the outward consequences were dysfunctional to live with. There was no rationality in this family and they couldn't see things as they really were. As a rational person, it nearly drove me mad dealing with them.

I spoke a completely different language to them and they were incapable of seeing anything from my point of view. My choice to marry into this family had inadvertently caused my son's death, and all the dreadful circumstances I had faced during my unhappy time with them.

My children from this marriage have elements of this illness in them and are genetically vulnerable. My eldest daughter especially does not have the capacity to see things as they really are and does not have the ability to see things from another people's perspective, and there was a cruel aspect to her character just like her father's. There were times when we also spoke a completely different language from one another.

She had a consistent habit of making assumptions which is the number one thing that creates unnecessary conflict in relationships. Assuming is a primitive impulse to make meaning unconsciously negatively focused, as a way to stay safe. If we can plug in our minds assumptions about the other person, their motives, and the reasons for what's happening, then we feel safe in a sense of knowing. Even if it's confabulated.

At one time, during a very stressful episode in her life, she confessed to me that she had heard voices in her head. We know that extreme stress can trigger the illness as well as the slings and arrows and misfortunes of life, and challenging circumstances. My mother-in-law's youngest son's illness had been triggered while he had been working in the bank as a young trainee and had been bullied by a woman manager who had made his life hell while working there because he was the boss' son.

There are striking similarities between my eldest daughter and her grandmother. My daughter also married into banking and has 3 sons of her own, a nice home and all the creature comforts and security that entails. She had picked up certain behavioural traits from her grandmother naturally because she spent a lot of her childhood around her.

We now know to a level of certainty that diagnoses such as 'bipolar disorder' and 'schizophrenia' are not separate conditions. There is no clear line between severe psychiatric disorders and healthy functioning, with the consequence that large numbers of people manage to lead productive lives despite experiencing symptoms at some time or another, and without seeking help.

My decision to allow my children access to their grandparents when they were young despite their father not being around, came about because I believed at the time that the stability the grandparents gave would help my children, but the reality actually was that I had inadvertently exposed them to an emotionally dysfunctional family, and because of this, they have some of these traits in them.

Also because my own parents were not around, there was no balance of the two families for my children to be exposed to. It was only ever one sided. Only by writing my memories in this book and doing the research into mental health illness do I see it all so clearly now, and shockingly, it is a sorry realisation that I have genetically passed on this debilitating disease to my children and grandchildren.

Why don't we do psychoanalyst work on an individual before we get involved in a relationship with them and a history of their family genetics? Perhaps this question is in another book.

If we don't understand our partner's childhood and current family dynamics, their core wounds, and the origin stories around their pain and patterns, we will have a hard time navigating our conflict differently and making long-lasting changes with each other. It is vital that we don't underestimate the importance of connecting to the richness and complexities of our partner's past and childhood.

The way their family operated carries a lot of weight. The way they communicated and fought matters. The beliefs that they held about people and the world matters. The things they prioritise matters. And maybe most importantly, the unresolved pain our partners holds with them is necessary for us to understand.

There is so much that goes into navigating relationships well, but there's also so much that makes it so difficult. So many of us jump into relationships based on sexual chemistry, appearances and financial advancement that we don't look at that person's background, childhood and cultural and social differences before we commit to that person.

As an empath, healer and compassionate individual, I knew I had to forgive this family for their short comings, especially after having done the research into mental illness, knowing that each individual is only trying to do their best with what life has thrown at them, but it's not easy being of the receiving end of a mental illness.

I had been given a clue by my mother-in-law many years earlier when getting into a debate about some behaviour, she had said to me, "Well, of course, you are perfect, aren't you?" I should, at the time, have recognised that comment and seen the psychology behind it, but of course, I was still in the infancy of my psychology knowledge.

My mother-in-law's behaviour towards me was probably a symptom of her upbringing and the experiences she had in her childhood, like so many of us we are all a product of this. Her constant need to elevate herself and her family in a prideful way and to block out mine as insignificant, probably derived from her childhood experiences of not being seen or heard by society and being rejected by it due to the social negative stigma her family would have faced due to the schizophrenia at that time in history.

Her husband's success in his career as a bank manager and his elevated position in society because of it, a member of the local rotary club, private golf club, RNLI and the local Royal Motor Yacht Club, all signs of a privileged and successful career would have elevated her within society and a high status and acceptance would have been achieved. This would have counteracted out any shame or negative experiences she would have faced in her childhood and was probably the reason why she was the way she was.

Try as she might though, she still couldn't escape the social prejudices, and stigma that society still puts on mental illness. Both she and her husband had been humiliated and embarrassed by it over the years in their youngest son but had played it down the best they could not wanting to draw too much attention to it.

In psychology, we look back at a person's childhood because as a child develops, more complex emotions such as confidence, hope, guilt, and pride emerge. Emotional development also includes a child's ability to feel and understand the emotions of other people through empathy. How a child observes and interacts with parents and care givers and the world around them affects their mental development.

Childhood has an effect on our adulthood and our early experiences shape our beliefs about ourselves, others and the world. Therefore, we learn rules to protect our self-belief as it may make us vulnerable. In doing this, we form dysfunctional behaviours, which then can lead to mental health problems.

My mother-in-law over the years would repeat the same conversation over and over again to her grandchildren, telling them she was very grateful for a good life—a life whereby she didn't have to worry about money and was kept in the lap of luxury and a privileged lifestyle. Out would come all the old photographs of her family and stories of the substantial land they had once owned and the farm in Jersey, and also her husband's Wilson Hat manufacturing industry back in the Victorian age.

She made out to them that she had an easy, good and uncomplicated life. She never discussed the schizophrenia, almost denied its existence and avoided discussion of it with them and never spoke about its implications during her young life. She only focused on the positive, privileged and material things she'd experienced while married to her husband, and the social standing she attained through it, as that was so terribly important to her.

I wondered why she was like that and so prideful because knowing her and her family for nearly 40 years, I knew this not to be the case. Her life had been over shadowed by the schizophrenia and it had been made hellish by it.

Delusional and in denial comes to mind…

Everything seemed to make sense now when I look back at my life spent with my first husband and the struggles I faced. It was my choice to engage in a relationship with them and enter into their world all those years ago. Naïve and as young as I was at the time, I had to except my uninformed choices I made and make peace with them.

Doing my research for this book has given me a greater understanding of this horrible debilitating illness and a window into the world of mental health illnesses and the stigma associated with them, and acknowledge fully that I had been a casualty of its side effects. Still today, nearly 40 years on, my first husband is still delusional and refuses to acknowledge the damage he inflicted on his children all those years ago or take any responsibility whatsoever for his actions.

I find it incredulous that his children have not challenged him on the subject and that he has not apologised to them.

I feel sorry for my second husband who had to pick up the pieces of such a dysfunctional family and had to take care of his stepchildren who had all been born with a silver spoon in their mouths with entitlement. This sometimes caused difficulties for him over the years due to their inherited illness and stubborn personalities.

He had financially cared for them and had provided them with a safe environment and happy home life, enabling them to grow into fully functioning members of society and had bestowed on them every advantage to be anything they wished themselves to be in life. Indeed, my girls had done exceptionally well in their education and chosen field of career, allowing them financial security in adulthood.

Today, I don't think they fully acknowledge his generosity and the extreme hard work it took him to take care of them as well as his own three children. My son was the only one who did voice and acknowledge this and he told me before he died that it was only Paul and I who had truly and fully ever helped him throughout his difficult life. Like my new friend, Terry, I am determined to have the last word and voice the injustice and unfairness of it all.

With my mother-in-law now dead, I wondered how her family would cope. She had been such a large figure in everyone's lives; with a powerful energy huge personality and presence and influence over them all. Her youngest son, now without a carer and in his 60s, was going to have to live and be looked after by his older brother and his wife. I had huge reservations about how that was going to turn out given my first husband's lack of patience and the inability to care for anyone other than himself.

At her funeral, being a public event, her grandchildren from her second son's first marriage would attend and have not had anything to do with their father since childhood, I could imagine the difficulties that would present, especially as that son had remarried and had gone on to have another two children of his own who did not know the existence of his previous children.

They say that it takes only two generations for a person to be forgotten. If you don't have a relationship with someone, how does their story continue on? How is it remembered, honoured, and integrated for the generations to come? Maybe it happens through storytelling, but who's telling the story and what parts are shared, known and deeply understood? I am not here to disrespect my mother-in-law's name or memory, but I am here to record what I did know about her and how my relationship was with her.

Understanding the stories of others is not meant to offer excuses. It is meant to offer context, and often context helps us connect to compassion, empathy and grace. It does not release accountability or responsibility, but it does paint a picture that can help our story make a bit more sense.

There is a complex, intricate and layered story to everyone's life and without getting deep and personal about that person, many of us will know very little about the complex, intricate, and layered lives of those people closest to us.

For example, I did not know my grandmother and grandfather on my paternal side and I struggled to tell anything at all about them. Of course, I had heard stories about them but what I know is very factual and detail-focused. I know less about their pain and wounds. I do not know what they were able to resolve or what was left unresolved emotionally before they died. Did they sit with their trauma or avoid it?

I don't know the grief they lived with or the way they expressed emotion, and I don't know the stories they told themselves about themselves that may have impacted their confidence, worth and the way they valued themselves in the world. So many of us try to heal our own pain without understanding the pain and context of those who came before us. All our ancestors since the beginning of life are alive and functioning as genetic and epigenetic activity in every cell of our bodies.

As I sit here and write these words, it has become clear to me that I am not interested in being remembered for what I've done or for what I have accomplished in terms of accolades. I am more interested in being remembered for what I healed internally. For the ways I moved through my pain and how I got there. I want that story be told to my grandchildren, my great grandchildren and the generations that follow.

I would like my story to inspire and I want what I don't move through to be understood also. Because that resolution will be passed down in some way, and the generations to come should know about it so that they can understand what part it plays in their own life story.

Chapter 4

On the 24 of February 2022, Russia began a military invasion of Ukraine in a major escalation of the Russo-Ukraine conflict that began in 2014. It was the largest military conflict in Europe since World War II. With over three million Ukrainians fleeing the country, the invasion caused the largest refugee crisis in Europe since the World War II. With Russia being such a powerful nation and owning nuclear weapons, the fear across the world was that Putin held the threat of nuclear destruction which threw us all into fear and panic.

I tried to look at the spiritual perspective on war and asked myself, 'What makes a person want to go to war?' After all, wars are started by individuals, and we know that we all have a shadow and light side to our personalities and human nature. Hitler and Putin were just individuals. Our need to destroy and our inherent nature to choose grace and the power of love are sometimes in conflict also.

Some of us go to war in our own personal lives. I have not met a person yet who has not waged a personal war against someone, divorce is often a battleground, as is a custody fight over children, Inheritance, money, and power struggles are another. Any issue that activates a sense of entitlement or injustice can begin a personal war, such as believing you were overlooked for a raise or promotion or indeed faced unfair dismissal.

The inability to forgive someone is, in fact, the choice to stay at war with someone, even if that war is fought through the use of silence. We have to face the fact that so long as we nurture vengeance or entitlement, anger or pride in ourselves rather than forgiveness and understanding, we will find ourselves on a personal battlefield time and again in our lives.

When you are hurt by something someone has said or done, it is common to want the other person to understand the impact and hear your pain. But when that person won't or can't for whatever reason, replace point proving, convincing, or trying to get them to validate you with you validating yourself.

There is nothing easy about forgiveness. I can tell you that from personal experience of events, not having a voice or being heard is one of the hardest things to experience. I have firsthand knowledge of what it feels like to not be understood or be told you think differently from everyone else. Coming across people who defend, skirt responsibility, manipulate or full-on shut down when you try and bring your opinion forward is hurtful and frustrating.

When attempts are blocked and you bent over backwards saying something a thousand different ways, yet are not being heard or understood, rather than causing a breakdown in relations, it has taught me it's better to go within myself to be heard, seen and acknowledged. More than anything, our system wants to be understood, go where it is honoured and there is healing.

Holding onto resentments only causes you pain and suffering internally and the other person invariably gets to walk away. For your own freedom, health and inner peace, it's important to let it go. We are the individual engines of what is created in this world, from our personal lives to the collective events that shape the world. Events do not just happen.

Consider the universal law that 'All Is One', all life breathes together. We now know from scientists that our world is interconnected, especially in nature and the animal world and our planet. As difficult as it is to imagine, our personal actions, in an energetic way, contribute to the collective energies of the whole of life.

We may think we live separate lives but that is a great illusion. If the pandemic did nothing else, it showed us and brought to our awareness how interconnected we all are. The energy that generates wars arises from the same cosmic truth that we are all connected. The war in the Ukraine, although we may think is far away and not in our country of liberty and freedom, it is still connected to our planetary community.

We may suffer from petrol prices from the knock-on effect of the war and be mildly inconvenienced, but nothing compared to Ukrainians losing their homes and their lives. Make peace everywhere in your own life. If you don't think one person can make a difference, think again. This war was started by one person—Putin.

One person has started a war of pain and untold suffering to many, never underestimate the power of your soul and every choice that you make to make an impact in this world.

On my days off from work and at the weekends, I would drive out to the East Sussex countryside and walk in its glorious surroundings in the Area Of Outstanding Natural Beauty to ponder life and try and make sense of this crazy world we live in. The High Weald that runs into neighbouring Kent and the chalky white hills of the South Downs were as beautiful as the other parts of the UK where I had been fortunate enough to live.

The southeast coast was easily accessible from London by road and rail, and offered a mixture of coastline, chalky hills and rolling downs, including the Weald. Bordered by Surrey, Kent, West Sussex and the English Channel where the coast offers panoramic views of the sea, with the famous sheer cliffs of Beachy Head, 162 metres high, part of the rugged cliff formation.

The East Sussex coast had been the scene of many invasions and the historic castles, including Bodiam, Pevensey, Herstmonceux, Lewis, reflect the battles of the past. The town of Hastings was the site of the 1066 Battle of Hastings, where Battle Abbey now stands. The ruins of the Norman-built Hastings Castle, once home to William the Conqueror, stared out to the English Channel.

The seaside resort of Brighton is popular with day trippers where the Royal Pavilion, beach front, pier, nightlife and lanes, provide great entertainment.

I would focus my walks in a village called Mayfield only 10 minutes away by car. Mayfield and Five Ashes were located in the High Weald Area of Outstanding Natural Beauty. Perched on the top of one of the east-west ridges with views of the north and south. The countryside was made up of scattered woods and shaws, irregularly shaped fields and small farms.

Many signs of its habitation over the centuries were visible as you walked along its many paths and bridleways with sunken tracks as well as mounds and ditches indicating ancient boundaries. The High Weald harboured such rare species as the of dormouse, the pearl bordered fritillary and black headed cardinal beetle. Nightjars bread in the open space created when woodlands were actively worked. The ancient woodland ground flora was species rich and included coral root bittercress, another speciality of this area.

In spring, the birdsongs were delightful with chiffchaff and great tits singing; a good time to spot birds as they sing to attract their mates and protect their territories. I could hear great spotted woodpeckers from the nearby woods as they pummelled the tress with their machine gun sound high up in the canopy. Country lanes and trails full of splashes of colour from spring flowers such as daffodils, lesser celandine and primroses.

Butterflies such as the brimstone, a big yellow variety with wings that are shaped to look like leaves, also peacocks and red admirals. On a sunny spring morning, this could fill your senses with such joy.

The Weald supported 1,400ha of unimproved grassland habitat, nearly 20% of the entire resource of lowland meadow in England.

Mayfield was close to Tidebrook, a little hamlet in a valley connecting the two villages and the home of the Old Rectory where I had once lived and raised my children with Paul for ten years and was next door to our dear little church. Some say that life comes full circle and it seems this has happened to me. My son, Daniel's, ashes were buried in the churchyard and it was the place where my brother, Andrew, had come to find me before he had taken his own life.

My walks would be proceeded with a visit there to pay my respects. The area still felt like home to me and I was drawn to it regularly. Paul's father's ashes had been scattered in the little copse wood that had once belonged to our land and a bench had been placed there in honour of him.

I was starting to accept and embrace my life as a single person now, rejecting any stigma associated with living and being alone. My work was to shift from 'I don't want to be single' to 'my single feels so good that I'll only trade it for something that feels just as good as if not better'. From the age of 21 years, I have spent a lifetime caring for others, always looking out for everyone outside of myself.

I wanted to do this as it was in my nature to do so, but now I recognised the importance of not overlooking myself first. A cup is just a cup if it isn't overflowing; you have to spoil yourself, not just financially, but with the peace of mind that comes with not bearing everyone else's stress and responsibilities.

A stable me was beneficial to everyone and a thriving me was essential in this path of liberation. I just needed to work on the prosperity. I was finding huge peace and comfort and meaning in my solitude and was in no rush to find a life partner. I wanted to make my alone sacred and special and learn to love it. It could be just as beautiful as any partnership.

I found listening to my own uninterrupted thoughts and trusting my own judgements was paying off. Indeed, after two decades of someone else making all the decisions, disregarding my opinions and controlling every aspect of my life, now relying on my own choices and decisions was revolutionary to me.

I didn't recognise the girl who wrote her first book *The Journey*. When I read it, occasionally it makes me cringe. I moved on so quickly once I had my financial independence and started writing my books and doing my healing work. It all seemed preposterous that I spent years replaying the same old movie over and over again in my mind of the past, the negative attachments continuously playing out.

I am able to remain calm and completely in control now because I am aware and able to let go and release. This calling was my greatest power and freedom of choice to decide deeply and truly what was right and best for me. My life within myself. Those memories, scenes and issues that had been bothering me for so long, I could completely let go of now.

As my unconscious mind kept replaying it, it now looked like visiting an old video back in time, a worn-out version of me. I no longer was that person. I had outgrown her. I no longer related that way. Old actions and old behaviours did not represent me now. That movie was so outdated. All those scratch marks, dust, and glitches had turned it into an old-fashioned image.

Sometimes out of loneliness, we can choose a partner for all the wrong reasons and after everything I had learnt, I was determined not to do this again, and so I embraced the quietness and calm and kept moving forward little steps at a time.

Osho writes, 'The capacity to be alone is the capacity to love. It may look paradoxical but it is not. It is an existential truth that only those people who are capable of being alone are capable of love, of sharing, of going into the deepest core of the other person, without possessing the other without reducing the other to a thing and without becoming addicted to the other.

'They allow the other absolute freedom because they know that if the other leaves, they will be as happy as they are now. Their happiness cannot be taken by the other because it is not given by the other.'

I was continuing to explore the human relationship and the complexities of them. How do I have better boundaries? How do I handle conflict with grace and discernment and love and still be fierce? And how do I navigate all this complexity of the world right now while all the time being a human, which is hard? Being in this dirty dance with life and other flawed humans, makes life beautiful when you can unwind it and see all of the different emotions that come forward are beautiful.

Being able to learn from them and keep taking a step forward every day was my journey and work. There were more moments when I realised I was no longer the same person. Life had changed. The me before had slowly faded in the fabric of the years. If I look closely, the scars are still there but they no longer cause me pain. Now they are simply part of my story. Instead of being something I ran away from, they have now become something that has created the strength in who I am now.

Sometimes we hold on to certain people because we think we have to. We put up with the emotional abuse, with all the bullshit they give us, with all the pain they've inflicted, and still, we hold on because we think we have to because we'll feel bad if we decide to let go and move on as we have so much history together and because we're afraid of being alone. Sometimes we hold on for the wrong reasons, for reasons we can't even understand ourselves.

We hold on to the point where our hearts bleed and bruise…but there comes a time when you must ask yourself why. Why are you still here? Why do you take this abuse? Why do you stay when you know things can be better? Why? You are a lover, you are a believer. And I know you want to believe that they will change but let me tell you from my experience, they won't. Deep down, you know they won't.

You gave them chance after chance and things just went back to the way they were. Things stay the same and it hurts. I know because I've been there. It's time to move on from all the things you've held on to. All the people who have caused you more harm than good. It's time to give up on them, it's time to move on…

By March, the country was getting back to normal after 3 years of disruption and mayhem caused by the Corona Virus and around this time, it was my youngest daughter, Summer's, 16th birthday. My youngest child and the last in the nest after having raised 7 children since the age of 22 years of age. A beautiful soul who had never given her father and me any cause for worry, who had never caused chaos or been unkind in any way. She had been an angel to raise.

I know that we as parents are not supposed to have favourites in our children, but I loved her differently from my other children and had a strong soul connection with her.

I had not seen my stepchildren properly since I had separated from their father and although, Paul kept me updated on their progress, I missed them. I wondered how I would be received by them at my youngest daughter's birthday celebration dinner and if would they take their father's side and be overly protective of him, or would there be any animosity towards me and awkwardness like divorces sometimes cause.

All now fully grown adults with busy lives and careers of their own and with partners themselves, it was hard to get them all together under one roof. My middle daughter, April, attended too. Obviously, my son, Daniel, was not there in person but I believed he was in spirit.

My eldest daughter and I had not spoken since falling out over my flat, but on this rare occasion, it was a wonderful feeling seeing them all gathered for Summer, and it reminded me of past memories when we had all been a cohesive family unit full of love, fun and belonging to one another in our home at the Old Rectory.

The evening was spent catching up on recent news and relaying sentimental stories of them as children and watching their reactions to their youngest sibling as they joked and teased her was very touching. There were lots of laughter and happiness. The love and affection from them towards me was still very evident and afterwards, I felt a huge sadness and void in my heart saying goodbye, not knowing when I would see them all again. I love them all dearly.

It was evident that they still all saw themselves as a family and I knew that when Paul and I were no longer around, they would continue to be a strong family unit and watch out for one another. Paul and I consciously uncoupling and remaining respectful, the friendship we continued to have towards one another, and how we had raised them had paid off well it seemed.

It was to be a double celebration as my eldest step-son, Thomas, would be leaving his job in London at Cartier to become an apprentice on the Isle of Man to the famous watch maker RW Smith. The world's greatest living watch maker RW Smith had been trained by George Daniels.

These two extraordinary men became the world's greatest living watch makers and my step-son who had studied horology at Birmingham School of Jewellery was to be their next apprentice. There had been a compelling film made about their extraordinary craft, touching relationship, and unique personalities of these two men.

The film highlighted the obsession, passion, personality, and perseverance, and was about the passage of time, making every moment count, about life and ultimately, about death, and Tom was about to become a part of all of that. Naturally, his father and I were incredibly proud of his accomplishments.

Having to accept that we were technically a broken family now was incredibly sad. My whole life had been a consistent story of loss and endings and I have never managed to escape the pain associated with that and I don't think I ever shall despite trying so very hard to transcend it. Try as I might to bring peace, love and forgiveness into my own personal life while contemplating a reconciliation with my husband, consequently hoping to procure a stable family life was proving difficult.

Despite offering love and forgiveness for his past demeanours, it had come to no avail and we continued to remain just friends and live apart. This transient life that was destined for me must be because of the contract I had made in heaven before I chose to come and live this human experience. It was perhaps a most cruel and brutal one but maybe I had to trust that the universe had other plans for me.

Every moment in our lives is deeply meaningful and plays a significant part of our personal journey. A lot of time we judge the moment because things don't go our way, but if we looked at life backwards, we would perhaps understand that those moments made us evolve and brought a shift in our consciousness. Whatever we are going through right now will not make sense to our human mind; we can't comprehend the divine order of the universe through logic.

Sooner or later, I guess that the dots will add up and connect and we shall realise that everything was preordained all along. Higher consciousness is all about trusting the divine order of the universe and seeing the deeper truth in every moment. Trust can only come from a place of surrender. Surrendering doesn't mean you let go of free will, it simply means you let go of the things that are not under your control.

As humans, we tend to look back at life through rose-tinted spectacles, there's such a strong tendency to believe that things *could* have been different. And worst still, that they *should* have been different. This only creates resistance to life and has us literally fighting against life and reality, which of course is a losing battle. Things are the way they are. It is our own perception of life that has us internally in a state of unease about it which creates our own suffering.

What if we could not only recognise things *are* the way they are right now, but also be totally okay with that? Feeling okay with how things are in the present moment brings peace to the body. This is not about resignation or apathy, or saying that things are ideal, easy or in any way perfect. But that does not deny the fact that they are nonetheless the way they are. I was still desperately committed to trying to create a life I wanted.

But as it relates to my history, accepting that things could not have been different and truly accepting that, rather than dragging it around with us, is one of the most freeing things one can do for yourself. What happened happened, and couldn't have happened any other way…because it didn't.

At the end of April 2022, I was contacted via the online dating site by a lovely gentleman living in Bedfordshire who's profile stated that he was a lover of travelling and was looking for a lady to share love, companionship and travels. He had been married for forty years to the same woman but sadly, she had died of cancer a year before after being ill for a long time. He had 4 grown-up children and it was clear that we both shared a common suffering of grief.

In his 60th year, he was a kind, considerate man, and despite a career in finance, was a conscious man. The attraction was instantaneous for me. He was so genuine and respectful, empathetic and compassionate, principled with a moral compass. We talked via WhatsApp video call and, then after several calls, decided to meet.

He came to Tunbridge Wells to see me and we had lunch in a smart restaurant then afterwards, I took him to Hever castle whereby we stayed there walking, talking and enjoying each other's company until it closed. I was delighted to see that he was tall, blonde, and handsome, greying slightly, and appeared to be a beautiful human being. Had I finally met my soulmate? We continued to text each other every day after that and we met up again in London for a second date which was a halfway commute by train for us both.

We spent the day sightseeing. He had organised all the proceedings as a surprise for me. So kind and thoughtful. We started by visiting the Tower of London then lunch on Tower Bridge, a boat ride on the Thames and then finally, the

London Eye. A full and exhausting but exhilarating day, and I enjoyed every moment.

The following weekend, we arranged to go away for a couple of days together. In hindsight, perhaps too early given we had only just met, but we were enjoying ourselves enormously and shared so much in common. He was so easy and comfortable to be with.

Again, he was to surprise me with having organised the few days away which coincided with the platinum jubilee celebration of our reigning monarch Queen Elizabeth the second. I found myself yet again being taken back to the Cotswolds, this time to Broadway where we were to stay in a hotel called the Lygon Arms and explore the Cotswold villages surrounding the area. I was very apprehensive about sharing a room with him, although he did give me the option of having my own hotel room.

He was so respectful and such a contrast to the other fleeting men I had met on the dating website. He had booked a twin bedded room and was a gentleman the entire visit. I was not ready for intimacy. The emotional abuse I had suffered with my previous marriages had left me somewhat damaged and time and trust had to be earned. We could speak about this openly together and he was happy to wait until I was ready.

After spending a weekend of quality time together and being treated like a princess, it was time to say goodbye and get back to work as I had to resume my childcare work commitments. With him being retired and in a comfortable financial position and not needing to work, both our worlds were to differ greatly.

Still I did not feel like the poor relation, instead I embraced my independence and continued on my path of focus and manifestation of what I had planned to achieve. I was not going to fall into the trap of my past needing a man to take care of me. I had come such a long way on my healing journey.

He sent messages to me stating what a lovely kind person I was and that he was falling for me and that I was what he had been searching for. I, unfortunately, did not fancy him in the same way and I knew unless I was able to overcome the damage done by my previous relationships and be able to resume intimacy, it could compromise things.

Sadly, after what was becoming a relationship via daily WhatsApp messaging and the inability to meet up due to my work commitments and his freedom to travel as and when he liked and with his fully booked up social diary of events, the relationship fizzled out. What was positive about it all though, and definitely evident, was that I was now attracting the right kind of soulmate and it would be only a matter of time before the right one presented itself.

The summer months passed quickly and work was very busy. I started to hear regular comments from the parents I worked with of 'professionalism' and 'excellence'; also great reviews about my services were being written on my online childcare app. My childcare business was thriving and doing very well indeed and I was proving to be in high demand.

At the end of June, my daughter completed her GCSE exams at school and it ended a chapter in our lives whereby finally I had provided a stable and safe environment for her to do so, and any memories of our time homeless and stuck out in Spain when we thought we would never get back to the UK, all the while her education being compromised, was firmly put in the past.

It had now been three years that I had been living on my own without any chaos or drama caused by my husband, my older children, or any others outside of the home. All seemed to be going well. Finally, there was continuity, peace and stability, and I was proud of this moment and of what I had achieved.

In August, Paul, Summer, and I took a well-needed holiday back to Southern Spain where our adventures of living in rural isolated nature in the mountains of Murcia had started five years previously, and where the content for my writing had been inspired from, where we had our romantic and challenging experiences with Spain, the memories of which were to stay with us all a lifetime.

We had met friends in Andalusia while we had been living there and had kept in touch over the years, making it possible to secure accommodation on a mates' rate basis, allowing us a more economically viable holiday and a much-needed break. The three of us had not seen much of one another over the summer months due to distance and work commitments, so a trip together was much-needed family time. It felt like going home as we caught up with old friends and frequented old familiar places and habitats.

The sunshine and starched big blue skies, that boast 325 sunny days each year, made Spain an ideal all year round destination. It reinvigorated us as we went about our business. The fearsome Iberian summer with its heat of 40 degrees and rising temperatures didn't hinder our lust for adventure and the outdoors.

We explored medieval towns on land, particularly UNESCO world heritage sites, as well as the costal resorts and beaches we knew so well. Paul as ever was great at researching places worth a visit, and his navigation and driving skills made for a very pleasant holiday indeed.

The medieval town of Ubeda in the province of Jaen in Andalusia was a town on the southern ridge of the so-called Loma de Ubeda, a table sandwiched in between the Guadalquivir and the Guadalimar river beds. It was one of the Andalusia jewels in the crown, an elegant and cultural town. As a UNESCO world heritage site, it listed an early example of Renaissance civic architecture and is an easy drive from Granada, Jaen, Carmona and Seville.

We had an evening meal in its Parador Hotel, a 16th century palace, originally built for Fernando Ortega dean of Malaga Cathedral but he died before it was completed sadly. It's located next to the Pantheon, one of Ubeda's most impressive sights.

Inside, it was filled with genuine antiques and the spacious entrance opened onto a Juliet balcony overlooking a quiet courtyard with water fountains and foliage. We explored the magnificent cathedral and churches and even a medieval synagogue pre-circa 1319.

The area is also famous for the growing of olives and the production of the finest extra virgin olive oil. The journey down had been a site to behold as we passed through hundreds of olive groves as far as the eye could see, so pretty and lush landscape. The Embalse del Negretin in the Cuevas del campo region, the third biggest lake and reservoir in Andalusia, was a vivid turquoise marine vast expanse of water situated with a mountain backdrop, which had stunning vista.

We caught up with old friends and as usual, we all got on famously and bonded in our past shared experiences of the country. The familiar mountains I adored so much instilled in me a feeling of energy and wonderment, and made me feel at home there. Two weeks passed quickly and blissfully. To conclude our holiday, we decided we would make a trip to Lorca, the city in the region of Murcia, back to the mountains and Marcos Estate La Parrilla, to see if much had changed since we had last lived there.

The three of us were emotionally attached to the place as all of us had such fond memories of that time spent there together, despite being technically homeless at that time. With Marco now living and working back in England and the estate up for sale, it would be interesting to see how the place was doing.

The drive up the mountain still had us in awe and wonderment at its beauty. It had not changed since we were last there, and in some way, because it was such a familiar place to us, it was somehow more staggeringly beautiful than before. The countryside was quaint, speckled with castles, aqueducts, ancient ruins and market gardens full of character as we ascended the mountain.

The familiar piggeries along the route that produced the famous Jamon Iberico ham, which were being built while during the time of living there, were now finished and were smartly painted buildings, but the hydrogen sulphide smell of the pigs was a cocktail of odorous gases and organic compounds in which higher concentrations of it were potent and as unpleasant a smell as we remembered.

The bins outside on the road were now covered and we did not see any of the usual wild cats with green eyes in and around them. The centuries old olive and almond groves that surrounded the area were carefully trimmed and the ground neatly cultivated with the backdrop of the brown rugged mountains in contrast behind them, dotted with palm trees and the remnants of their Moorish past. It was such a pretty landscape, especially while all of this was bathed in the most glorious sunshine.

After half an hour of driving, we finally arrived at the top of the mountain where we took the familiar and long unmade track that took us to Marco 700 hectare estate. Wild blackberries brambles over hung the track, sparkling but innocent, tangled thorny, and perhaps nature's most unassuming of gifts laden with fruit with flavour so sweet and aromatic. We could see from this that nature was now untamed.

The track bent and twisted itself up the mountain, avoiding pot holes and thick vegetation, the pine forest surrounding us on both sides, a pine-clad haven of cool in the summer and a glorious place to enjoy a walk and the home to a wide range of wildlife, especially the bird life with its great tits, crossbill finches and long-tailed tits, as well as its mammals such as the wild boar.

The predominant species of pine we passed were the Aleppo pine, and the European black pine which was home to this incredible bird life. We finally arrived at Marco's estate. On arriving, we were shocked and surprised to see what greeted us as the Cortigo had been neglected and appeared left uncared for. It was looking very down at healing and forlorn, if not pretty much desolate and deserted.

The sand, cement and lime rendering on the Cortigo buildings were looking in need of attention and repairs. Now stained yellow with cracks and holes appeared all over the properties, and with nature totally overrunning the buildings, weeds and tall grass and debris smothered what was once manicured and lovingly tended buildings that we had maintained.

The elation of once again seeing the breathtaking views from the high elevation, the beauty of which had me in tears. The nature here was honest and had such pure energy. It was a place to be in harmony; it was still the same stunning vista I had remembered so well and that I am ever unlikely to forget.

Surrounded by the great pine forest that cloaked the Penarrubia and Calo de los Enamorados Mountains as far as the eye could see, and those forests that we had walked in and explored five years hence, the walks that had compelled us to tread a landscape slowly to smell its different soils and immerse ourselves in its uniqueness and nature.

We saw the panorama of fertile plains below and the city of Lorca far in the distance. Gulping the fine dry air and sniffing the pitch pine mountain, made me feel so alive.

The house further down the track that had housed up to 13 guests in its day, that we had taken so much care of, in listing our time and energy making it look presentable for guests, had become unloved, ignored, shabby, empty, and a sorry excuse for itself. The swimming pool that Paul had so diligently looked after attaining crystal clear water was now empty and dirty with over grown shrubbery shrouding it.

Our memories of the place were shattering. The red orbs slashed with magenta and crimson of the pomegranates that we once picked fresh off the trees and had eaten with delight as the blood-red juices dripped drown our chins, and which at the time had symbolised life, love and vitality, were now smothered by long grass and strangled by weeds and now symbolised blood and death.

It soon became evident that our time here had been a rare period indeed. A period never to be repeated, and that although we were under difficult circumstances at that time, we had actually made a huge difference to the estate and to our own lives and Marco. The raw nature and isolation of the place had wrapped me in its loving embrace, protecting me, healing me after the death of my son and giving me back a reason to carry on living, reminding me of life and nature at its basic level and the inevitable circle of life.

By tending to and taming the land and its houses, we had brought the estate alive by putting all our energies and hard work into it. We had loved it as our own, and without us there anymore, it felt lonely broken and forlorn as if it had died and retreated into its isolated abyss once we had left. Nature can have more power over a person and is a threatening force to contend with, and despite humans making their stamp on it and taming it, nature will always outlast everything and here certainly was the proof of that happening.

After half an hour of looking around the estate, we left with feelings of sadness, nostalgia and sentimental longing for the broken and bittersweet past. Sometimes you have to treat nostalgia like a guest that is in danger of over staying its welcome.

In silence, we sat in the car with our thoughts as we headed towards Alicante Airport, a 2-hour drive to drop the hire car off and for our flight back home to the UK, knowing that as with everything in life, there is always a time and a place. By going back, we had finally ended that chapter in our lives. With new beginnings very much ahead of us all, we knew that we would probably never return to that part of Spain again.

Soon after our return from Spain at the end of August 2022, it was announced in the news that Prime Minister Boris Johnson was to resign and a new prime minister was to replace him. Boris Johnson had lost the support of his fellow MPS earlier in the year due to a number of incidents that had accrued. Our third women prime minister was to be the conservative Secretary of State for foreign commonwealth and development affairs, Elizabeth Truss.

On travelling to Scotland to meet with the queen at Balmoral Castle, where for the first time the queen had appointed a prime minister in Scotland because our sovereign was experiencing episodic mobility issues, she was the last prime minister to be appointed by Elizabeth III Queen of England as sadly at the age of 96, on the 19 of September 2022, our Queen died, and our country and the world immediately went into mourning.

Our country soon was to refer to our most affectionately respected sovereign as 'Elizabeth the Great' for she was the longest reigning monarch of the United Kingdom of Great Britain in its history, her 70 years on the throne was now to be a vanished era. A state funeral was to be arranged. This being the first time, certainly in my lifetime, I was to experience such a momentous event.

London suddenly became the centre of the world as heads of states from dozens of countries were to witness funeral rites and flummery in Westminster Abbey, while a billion or more of their citizens watched at home. Our new monarch was now King Charles III, who would carry on the continuity and tradition that his mother, our queen, had shown him.

A few weeks after this, my landlord announced that she was selling her property, and therefore, unless I wished to purchase it, I would be moving out. Also despite our lovely holiday break away in Spain with Paul and our daughter, Summer, on our return home, my ex-husband suddenly became withdrawn and standoffish, commenting that I was too friendly and that our friendship was not appropriate and conducive to being separated, and that appropriate detachment behaviour was necessary and was required from both of us moving forward.

It had come out of the blue and had somewhat been a shock that had thrown me. I felt that we had handled our separation maturely by consciously uncoupling and remaining friends all the while setting a good example to our children on how to be civil despite our differences and they had accepted this. Therefore, it had been rather a huge disappointment and upset to me that the dynamics were to change. Still, I had to respect his need to move on with his life without me.

I understood and believed that when a soul has completed its contract with another, the energy ends the relationship on its own accord. Sometimes life helps this end of the contract through an accident or an incident. Sometimes people try in vain to cling to another who is liberated from their karma or their mission. They desire again and again to receive attention from the first without understanding that it is over and they of course suffer.

Whether in friendship, as a couple, at work, in association, for humanitarian purposes, when the contract expires or in other words, when the lesson has been learnt from that circumstance, it is null and void and it is good to then move on. Pleas, requests for forgiveness, remedial attempts, accusations or tenderness are useless.

What was once right at one time is no longer right and it is a gift to be able to understand this, to accept it, and to evolve by moving on to other relationships adjusted in the energy of the present moment as this avoids resentment, sadness or, sometimes as we can see in very sad miscellaneous events, revenge, which in turn creates suffering for entire families and a much greater karma.

Hopefully, peace of mind sets in and with it peace of heart.

The greatest gift you can give someone is your own personal development. I used to think that if I took care of you, you would take care of me. Now I think differently and believe that if I take care of myself for you and you take care of yourself for me, then this is a much healthier relationship option.

As sad as all this was at the time, and before it all happened, I had known that a shift was coming. Being an intuitive person, I sensed that a change and new chapter in my life was about to come to fruition. I felt it in my gut and so while it was upsetting, it did not surprise me at all as I was somewhat prepared for it.

It was to be a stressful time though as I explored alternative accommodations for my daughter and myself while still having to navigate my ex-husband, personal finances, and work. I braced myself for this next stage. This is how life is it seems, a continual series of challenges and changes to overcome.

At this time, the country was under huge pressure as a 'cost of living crisis' was taking hold of the country and interest rates were escalating daily. Our new prime minister had resigned after only 45 days in office making her the shortest serving PM in UK history.

By radically reorienting the government's economic agenda, by slashing taxes without saying how the decision would be paid for, it immediately sent the British pound valuation falling and the central bank was forced to raise interest rates to 3% and the cost of taking out mortgages soared. Inflation already at a record high, raised the cost of living further and Truss never recovered.

Despite my immediate situation, there was a positive side to it; this would be in actually a great time to save money if I didn't have the costs and overheads of renting a new property. Then my dearest middle daughter, April, who is a highly sensitive and beautiful soul, suggested Summer and I come and live with her and 'sit out' this economic difficult period by helping her by moving in and paying a nominal amount of rent to help contribute towards her now large mortgage.

She was not on a fixed mortgage rate at that time and the recent interest rates had sent her mortgage repayments sky-high. The split and break up with her boyfriend earlier in the year, who had now consequently moved out, was now causing her to manage a three bedroom house on her own and financially she was under pressure.

I now could afford to put money aside and finally had the opportunity to put savings away which could eventually go towards a deposit on buying my own house in two years' time. I had come out of my second marriage pretty much destitute due to my ex-husband's addictions and so was rebuilding my life completely from scratch financially.

I was starting all over again at 57 years of age which terrified me, but I had to stay positive as I had to remember that I was starting from an experience that was full of good and bad experiences that I could now use to reinvent and reimagine what the next chapter of my life would look like.

With two incomes now coming into her home, the pressure would be decidedly taken off for all of us and finally, with family pulling together and hunkering down through this difficult time, the future was looking better. Little women together taking on the world…

Also living with my daughter was going to be a lovely experience because we were both gifted with the similar personality trait of high sensitivity, which made us great communicators. HSP or Highly Sensitive Person was a term coined in 1996 by American clinical research psychologist Elaine Aron to describe the 20-30% of the population who process thoughts, feelings and sensory input more deeply than others.

Generally speaking, society often downplays or even disparages signs of sensitivity using labels like 'delicate' and 'easily hurt or upset' or 'deep'. But what about those qualities such as insightfulness, empathy and diligence? These go more hand in hand with sensitivity. My middle daughter, April, and I had inherited this trait and were struggling to be understood by our extended family and romantic partners.

During this time, we were able to emotionally support one another and explore and understand this trait more deeply.

Highly sensitive people tend to notice things in their environment that others may miss and will carefully consider the pros and cons before making decisions or taking action. As a result, we are usually intuitive, creative, empathetic, cautious and conscientious. We also consistently take in large amounts of information, including sensory factors such as sounds, touch and movement, which can cause overload in some cases.

However, these are broad ranges of characteristics and not all of us HSPs are alike. Being highly sensitive is not a disorder and many of us have different degrees of it. We are not introverts like most people think, like me, 30% of us are actually extroverts. Highly sensitive children are deep thinkers, creative, intelligent, and of course, empathic. They are the heart-centred leaders we need for our future.

Perception of sensitivity can vary in different cultures and communities. Many professions and life situations require a compassionate human being to be there—medical staff, for instance, teachers, therapists, spiritual leaders and those working with children being highly sensitive is an advantage. The world could learn a lot from us who have this personality trait. Certain jobs have empathy and care at their core.

In a society where 'output' and 'productivity' are in job descriptions, what about the importance of using language to describe the importance of sensitivity? We can start to change what we value as a culture. I was very much passionate about this and although, certain people around me did not fully comprehend this, I was determined to set an example of this belief and I wished that my ex-husband and other members of my family understood this trait better.

Being more attuned to your work situation and family and friends can be an incredibly helpful skill to have, and it's possible for non-HSPs to strengthen theirs because there is a sliding scale of experiences.

Over the twenty years of living and being in a relationship with my second husband, my sensitivity was regularly received negatively. In a world where it's generally believed that if you experience things more sensitively than others, then you might be doing something wrong, it can be hard to be a HSPs. As a result, I had tried in the past to change the way I was or the way in which I did things.

But if you have to moderate your own internal story of what you're feeling and experiencing, it can take up even more energy, as well as compromise your authenticity. HSPs are of great value to society, so having to change to fit in is not only psychologically compromising for HSPs, but for society too. Understanding that an effective group of people is made up of lots of different thinking types can be useful to any company or community because their audiences are made up of lots of different thinking types too.

When I look back at myself, especially in my 20s, I see how precarious my self-esteem was. It is painful to look back at myself and see this. Friendships I was willing to stay in that were not good for me, and romantic relationships that were not right for me. When I tried to talk about it at the time, the same old response would be 'you're too sensitive', so I would stay and think 'you're right, I need to stop being sensitive'.

My life, my relationships, and my choices are very different now. Back then, before this journey of awareness started, I thought that people needed to see me as strong and I thought that everyone else seemed fine and that it was me who responded to things differently, and so there must be something fundamentally wrong with me. I know now that this is not the case and what a life journey of learning and understanding this has been.

I don't think I will ever know what it is like to not have emotions and deep feelings. I have always been this way, when I feel nothing, I feel it completely. Oh, how fascinating and different we all are and how diverse the human species can be.

By now, it was November and as the month came and went, my book had still not been published, with an estimate of between nine months and two years to publish a book, it was a frustrating wait. The final book cover design was all that was pending so it was certainly getting closer to its launch date.

Christmas 2022 was in sight and was predicated to be a different scenario to the ones Paul, Summer, and I had spent together in the past few years, or so I thought. This time, I had to address and navigate Paul's outburst in wanting us to be less friendly with one another and more formal in attitude and behaviour. With Paul wanting a distinct shift in our relationship now, I could not see how spending time together with our daughter over Christmas was going to work.

So with much deliberation, I contacted him beforehand to express my worries about spending this cosy family time together in the intimacy of my new home. I now had April to think about, and I did not want any atmosphere in her house spoiling the festivities. Also, I felt I could not be anything other than my authentic self and if that meant being overfriendly, then so be it.

I was not prepared to put on a false act just to accommodate him. It seemed unfair to ask me to do so, and anyway, if my only crime was that I was 'too friendly', it seemed ridiculous to be getting stressed about it.

Surprisingly, he was rather shocked and upset at the thought of not seeing us on Christmas Day and proceeded to explain that maybe he had been 'hasty' in his comments and promised me that there would be no atmosphere and that things could return to how they were before, and that he was looking forward to spending this time with my daughter and myself. I accepted this perhaps knowing deep down that if he was not with us, then he might be spending Christmas alone.

Christmas turned out to be a magical festive holiday with Paul being as generous as ever, arriving with gifts, food and drinks. Having his step-daughter around, who was loving, affectionate and accommodating of him, proved that the mending and healing of past wounds within our family had finally secured good relations. It reminded me of happier times and memories of when the family was happy and all together.

For this short amount of time, we were a family unit once more and as old familiar sentiments arose, I felt that lovely warm feeling of togetherness. In fact, all four older siblings were engaged in seeing one another over the Christmas period too—proof that despite our separation, the 6 children continued to be close and very much connected to one another.

With a new baby arriving in April of the following year, there was a feeling of excitement in the air as Paul's daughter was to make him a grandfather for the very first time.

Chapter 5

January 2023 started with a new 6-month nannying contract for an Australian/ British family and I threw myself into my new position. The new year can sometimes bring up painful and complex emotions for many of us, making us miss those who are not with us anymore and reminisce about how things used to be, which can be difficult to deal with, causing loneliness and anxiety which sometimes can bring on a depression.

If only I had a crystal ball and could see the future, know what the universe had in store for me and what it was doing to support me, and how all my hard work was paying off in ways I could not yet perceive. Hopefully, one day, I would step back and finally see clearly how the tangled knots of my unique path unravelled in divine timings—never too early, never too late.

How it would all unfold perfectly to lead me somewhere even greater than I had ever imagined. This hope and belief was what kept me going on my journey into the new year. To, eventually, see the magic that created my life. The beauty in the messiness and the richness of my everyday world in all of its glorious colours.

I would see how every long night and every early morning, every yes and every no was all for a reason. How it all would mean something in the end. I now recognise how some paths had to end so that others could begin, and how I had to climb the tallest mountain before I could soar. Until that day arrived when all this would unfold, I just had to hope that better things were ahead of me and that I was stronger than any challenge that came my way. This hope encouraged me to keep going.

I was really starting to enjoy my work as I met new and different people and the opportunities they presented. I found myself moving more into a child psychologist role as I was able to use the knowledge I had gained to help families with neurodiverse children and also help support parents in all kinds of family matters. It gave me huge insight into the human experience and how unique, unusual and varied people's lives were.

My mission was to make sure that the children I looked after got the best possible parenting experience to support their growth in a healthy and positive way.

I would collect children from the private schools that my own children and stepchildren had once attended and found myself reminiscing. If only I knew while I was on that sports field cheering on my children at the time, that ten years later my life would take such a drastic turn and all that was to happen to me. All the lessons that I still had to learn about life and its people, it would seem so inconceivable in that moment.

Perhaps a crystal ball was in fact not such a good idea after all. We are not meant to see the future. While most of the laws of physics are time-reversible, entropy is not, it only travels from past to future. As do our experiences.

Sometimes I wonder what the world would be like if we all knew our future. Perhaps it would be a boring world as to whether we are in a state of heaven or hell. As if we were a program and some programmer had written out a code for us. We would not have 'free will'. Why would we want that when we don't need to make a decision? When everything has been decided for us, what fun would it be to live such a life?

Every part of us would have been predetermined, such as meeting people, doing business, earning money, death, and there would never be any change in them. Would this not put a damper on everything life stands for? Still, a lot of us want to know what the future holds and sometimes we look for someone who can predict our lives. Only the institutional dreams, actuarial predictions, investment and insurance exist here.

As a species, we want to know the future because we are afflicted with uncertainty. We are in a world obsessed with predictions. We want to chart everything beforehand, every journey, every outcome and every step in life. We want to strangle every possible amazement this life has to offer. Psychologists believe insistence on knowing the future is connected to the control over certain things, events, and outcomes in our life and fate.

It leads to the question of our survival, which is related to evolution. The less we know, the more threatened we feel, because lack of knowledge means we do not know what we need to protect ourselves, meaning lack of control over health and safety, life and death. Knowledge is power over how things turn out.

It seems that we never care for the future when we are happy. We only embark on a journey for knowing the unknown future whenever we face troubles. No one knows what is going to happen at any given time in the future. It would help if we focused, therefore, on what is happening right now in the present moment. Every step of ours will pave the way we want our future to be.

Somethings we actually benefit from, like shocks and surprises because we can, in fact, thrive and grow when exposed to volatility, randomness, disorder, and stressors, and love adventure, risk and uncertainty. My own experiences of these things happening to me have led me to this growth and become a better version of myself than I ever would have thought possible. I would not be the person I am today without the lessons learnt from these past traumas and experiences.

While there have been times when I wished I could go back and change certain things from the past, I realised that every experience, both good and bad, played a crucial role in shaping the person I am today. Through the ups and downs, the twists and turns, it has helped me discover the strength within myself to overcome any obstacle. The past cannot be changed, and that's okay.

Because even when the journey was tough, and the road ahead was rough, I was able to see the light. The past has been my guide. The pain, the joy, and the love that grew along the way has been a journey that inspires me to keep going.

What I discovered, which is possibly the hardest part of life, is to teach our body emotionally what the future will feel like ahead of the actual experience. So what does that mean? You can't wait for your success to feel empowered, you can't wait for your wealth to feel abundance, you can't wait for your new relationship to feel love, or your healing to feel whole. That's the old model of reality of cause and effect, waiting for something outside of us to change how we feel inside of us.

When we feel better inside, we pay attention to whatever caused it, but that means from a Newtonian world that most people spend their whole world living in lack, waiting for something to change outside of them. The Newtonian world is all about predictability.

In contrast, the quantum world of reality is all about causing the effect. The moment you start feeling abundant or worthy and you are generating wealth, the moment you feel empowered and you are beginning to step towards success, the moment you start feeling whole and your healing begins, and when you love yourself and you love all of life, you will create an equal and now are causing an effect.

I think that's the difference between living as a victim in your world, saying I am this way because of this person or that thing, or this or that experience, they made me *feel* this way. When you switch that around, you become a creator of your world and you start saying 'my thinking and my feeling is changing an outcome in my life' and now that is a whole different game.

By writing my memoirs and learning all of this, it has now shown me that previously in my life, I had sadly been a victim.

There is a difference between being a victim of an atrocity and existing in victimhood. Of course, absolutely dreadful, awful, terrible things do happen in this world and can happen to any human. But being a victim is different from remaining a victim. To continue to exist in victimhood indefinitely without movement, keeps you stuck and keeps you from an inner reconciliation and peace.

The terrible stuff that happened to me does not necessarily need to be forgotten, downplayed or ignored, or avoided and even minimised because honouring what happened is part of the healing journey and is required. But you cannot heal if you continue to exist in victimhood. You won't find peace, resolution or reconciliation within you if you are stuck there.

Victimhood can trap you in a cycle of seeking recognition and rumination. Acknowledging and witnessing from yourself or others always falls short because there is a constant seeking of that recognition, therefore it means that the acknowledgement and witnessing don't get received and processed.

We tell our stories to others time and time again, to as many people who will listen, without actually receiving the benefits that can be offered from those who can hold the space and connect deeply with our pain because they can't metabolise it.

Victimhood is a distraction from actually tending to our pain.

Every single thought that we think has a frequency so if we are thinking thoughts that are connected to emotions such as anger or frustration, pain or suffering, or guilt, those thoughts produce a slower frequency. And because they produce a slower frequency, it causes us to feel more like matter and less like energy. We have to, in this realm, manage our thoughts and awareness.

Every single emotion produces a frequency and the slower the frequency, even slower the vibration, the slower the outcome in manifesting 3 dimensional reality.

The faster the frequency, the more elevated the emotion, and the closer we are getting to the unified field. So if we tune into a frequency of wholeness and oneness, newness and wonderment, we become more aware of it and stay connected to it moment by moment.

As we begin to open our awareness and tune into this frequency, once we can feel it, once we can experience it, once we become more aware of it, every time we have an experience of it, we begin to lay down circuits in our brain to perceive more of it the next time. In a sense, we are wiring our brains to become connected to that invisible field.

If we want to create a new life, a new personal reality, we have to change our personality. This means that we need to start thinking about what we have been thinking about and change it. We begin by being conscious of our unconscious actions, habits and behaviours and modify them.

We have to then start looking at the emotions that we live by every single day that keep us connected to the past and decide to ourselves do these emotions belong in our future. Some people are trying to create a new personal reality as the same personality and that does not work, unfortunately.

We literally have to become someone else. So the principal of neuroscience is that nerve cells that fire together wire together. We keep thinking the same way, making the same choices, demonstrating the same habits, creating the same experiences that stamp the same networks of neutrons into the same patterns all for the familiar feeling called *you*.

They say if you do that for 10 years on end and another 10 years on end, you will begin to hardwire certain patterns in the brain that become our identity. By the time we are 35 years old, it becomes fixed. Psychology used to say that we could not fix that, but we now know that we can. Thoughts come from all sorts of places; they come from our ancestors and some are actually written into our genetic code.

We know, for example, if three generations ago, there was a traumatic event, then we are at a higher risk of anxiety disorders and depression. Thoughts come from the voices of our mother and father and from siblings and friends, also from music and the news we watch. They are all a lie. Just because you have a thought, it has nothing to do with whether or not it is true. We must not get attached to our thoughts. That is *not* a helpful thought.

The moment we decide to sit down and do the work, do something differently, we become untangled from those old programs that we were running 95% of the time.

While trying my hardest to rewire my thoughts and emotions, I now also believed in and was very much following the practices of spiritual love. A way of experiencing love that transcended the physical and emotional aspects of love and connected me to something greater than myself. It was a love that comes from a deep sense of connection to the divine, and can be experienced in many different ways, such as through prayer, meditation, or acts of service.

I was developing a practice of mindfulness and self-awareness by becoming more aware of my thoughts and thinking, emotions and behaviours. I was now able to identify patterns that had blocked me from experiencing spiritual love in the past. By cultivating more positive qualities such as gratitude, compassion, and forgiveness, it was helping me connect more deeply with others and with the divine.

Through acts of service and giving, and focusing on helping others by making a positive difference in their lives, I was tapping into a deep sense of purpose and connection that brought me closer to the divine. By serving others with love and compassion, I was experiencing the transformational power of spiritual love.

My commitment to inner growth and transformation and a willingness to let go of old patterns and beliefs of the past that were blocking me from experiencing the fullness of love, I was now allowing myself to push forward in a new way of attitude towards life and ultimately helping the world while doing so.

Elkhart Tolle tells us that we are not the thinker but the awareness behind the thought. If we watch the thought, feel the emotion, and observe the reaction, we don't have to believe them. Whenever we are able to observe our mind, we no longer are trapped in it. We are awareness. Ego implies unawareness. He says awareness and ego cannot coexist.

We can change the way our brain works and we do have power over the way our mind works. I was now defiant about what my past trauma had done to me emotionally and psychologically and I was determined to move forward and past it. I survived what had happened to me and I had a responsibility to heal myself and do the work to change myself so that I could be the happy and fulfilled person that I was born to be.

I stopped looking for a partner to provide for me, providing financially and being supportive. The most important relationship we have is with ourselves. Belief in ourselves, self-confidence, self-awareness, self-reliance, self-esteem and self-love. Love, trust and faith in oneself. If we want validation, then we give it to ourselves. Through my efforts and my attitude, I believed that I would now always have an impact on any given situation that I was faced with.

I could ask for help because I believe I deserved it. I could seek therapy because I believe I can heal. I could seek information. It all begins with *me*.

There are two kinds of prisons that we can sentence ourselves to—one is the physical stuff; the circumstances of our lives, the circumstances of our body, the circumstances of our unfair life. The second is the mental prison. People can do all sorts of things to us that are unfair, that are not safe or cruel. It's unfair because we did not deserve it but the real power we will always have is how we react to it mentally.

It begins with our mental attitude of our own ability to be able to fix it, about our ability to face it, to survive it and move past it and have the ability to have an impact on any situation we are faced with. The most important relationship we have is with ourselves. We have to give ourselves those things. To have our own back to take back our power. Healing means making whole.

Very often, it's confused with curing which brings in an outside medicine or surgery to interfere with our inner process. Healing allows our psyche to work with us to bring wholeness to our being and this was my work.

As the nature of how I earned my living and my journey continued in constant motion, I was now looking after school age children, providing wrap around care and support, and learning more and more about the human condition, especially how our lives derived from our childhood experiences.

As I watched each and every interaction that parents had with their children in their environment, I had the foresight to see how the negatives would pan out further down the line if not corrected, and I was able to intervene and give guidance towards more positive outcomes in the future. I felt passionate about this. I was giving a gift to humanity and felt that it was my calling to do so.

It was fascinating and terrifying to see how lovely, intelligent and interesting middle class families were missing huge issues in their children's lives due to being just too busy with work life. One 8 year old little boy was addicted to his tablet and video games. Although, his parents thought they were just cartoon-led, in fact they were classified as rated 18 content and shockingly inappropriate if not damaging to the child. This had gone unnoticed until I pointed it out to them.

Of course, in this fast-paced society, it is hard for us all to find stillness inside and many of us suffer anxiety and restlessness, while our brains are all the time overstimulated by external triggers. Sometimes we miss important signals and don't see what is staring us straight in front of our faces because of it. Our attention span seems to get smaller by the day.

I wondered if we were running away from ourselves while being addicted to the thrill of dopamine and trying to escape silence and reality. Sincere introspection is definitely needed to slow us down and the only thing that can truly nourish and help us make a substantial change within ourselves and to those around us, especially our children.

On another assignment, parents with a medical background in psychology were complaining about the unsociable behaviour of their 5 year old son who would not do as he was told and was running rings around them, were able to see, once I helped point it out to them, that there was in fact nothing wrong with their son. He was a gorgeous, loving, kind, generous and affectionate little soul and that it was the fault of their parenting.

It turned out that their extreme reactions against their own disciplinarian childhood backgrounds in the past had caused them to overcompensate the other way and parent with less discipline towards their son, allowing him freedom to do as he pleased including disabling boundaries, therefore causing their son to have these behavioural problems. I knew that not having limits sows the seeds of narcissism and entitlement.

It also encourages a child to think about the people and things around them as things that exist to meet their needs and give them what they want. Children without boundaries or discipline will get a rude awakening when they don't always get what they want. Children feel insecure when they don't have clear limits; boundaries give them a sense of security. Setting limits removes arguments, back talk and discussion.

Of course, children will always try to get their way, however, knowing what the boundaries are and being reminded of them when they try to test you helps cut down the amount of back and forth the child will create as they try to convince you to give them what they want.

I tried to reinforce to all the parents I worked with the importance of how parenting has a huge impact on a child's development and, that as parents, it takes skill to raise a child and that it is a huge responsibility towards our children to send them out into the world as fully functioning, happy and balanced adults.

A 7 year old empathic, highly sensitive, and kind little girl that I had looked after had sadly been manipulated, coerced and bullied for 3 years by another little girl at her school. The mother had tried in vain to get to the root of the problem and had talks with the other girl's mother to no effect.

The little girls appeared to be friends and were in the same class, but the little girl in question would confide to me about her so-called friend and tell me that she just could not escape this girl's company and that she had tried to do so on many occasions. When she tried to make a new friendship group to get away from her, the girl would follow and take over the games they played with the new group of friends.

This friendship group would then exit to escape the other girl's poor behaviour which consisted of needing too much attention, complete control of games and play, no care towards other's feelings, and a sense of self-importance. This left my little girl isolated with this girl.

This had gone on for well over the period of time I had left working for the family. A year later when I caught up with them, the same situation had not been resolved. My little girl by now had no other choice other than to accept her situation that she had been presented with and was to be held prisoner to this girl's company and the behavioural consequences they presented.

In her own words, she had said to me, "She won't leave me alone. There is nothing I can do about it, so I just have to get on with it." This situation made her isolated from her other friendship groups who would not play with the two of them. Also by now, she could not complain to her mother anymore about her circumstances because this other girl would make her life difficult with verbal abuse if her own mother had chastised her because of it. She was now effectively trapped with this 7 year old narcissist without any support.

At the age of 7 years old, a child develops very important traits. I worried that my little girl was being conditioned with a trait of having to accept poor behaviour from others and that she felt that she had no choice other than to accept this. Of course, tolerance is a good characteristic but she was starting to be programmed with the mindset that she was unable to get away from her situation with this girl's unreasonable and manipulative behaviour and had to accept her fate.

She was left without the freedom of choice or free will to run or leave such a negative social situation. I knew only full well how this would manifest in her relationships in the future as she grew up and how she would attract more individuals with that personality trait if she did not address it now. What she would be facing and what she would think she had no choice but to tolerate in her life was becoming her normal.

True narcissists prioritise their needs above anyone else's, which most often shows up as pushing boundaries or breaking agreements. They also have a lack of empathy and respond with criticism, anger, or defensiveness due to their sense of their own unreasonable high sense of importance. Once you understand these behaviour signals of a possible Narcissistic Personality Disorder, solutions can be found.

The difficulty is that in a child's development, it is in fact a normal and important part of the developmental process. A child can't be diagnosed with a Narcissistic Personality Disorder until they are older.

We all have narcissistic aspects to our personality that help build self-esteem and self-worth. The difference with NPD is that the person has a persistent way of constantly feeling wounded, wronged or victimised and cannot tolerate other's success when set alongside theirs. They do this to such an extent that they are always upset and can't sustain relationships that require them to give and take.

They are entitled and feel no shame in it. Because children's personalities are still forming, they can't be diagnosed. Many kids and teenagers go through phases of being self-absorbed and have an inflated sense of confidence or self-worth and can lack empathy for others due to their own needs being met.

Empaths like my little girl are emotional sponges who can absorb feelings from other people very easily. This can make them very attractive to a narcissist because they see someone who will fulfil their every need in a selfless way and will also forgive them easily. Empaths have a lot of compassion and understanding to give, while narcissists thrive on someone worshipping them. This is not a good match because empaths forgive everything a narcissist does.

This results in them being completely used and degraded while the narcissist creates more and more chaos.

You can now see how my little girl was trapped in this difficult and damaging social situation within her school life because of her personality traits. It now needed to be sensitively addressed if she was not to be affected further down the line in her life. She needed to be shown and taught boundaries so that she *did* have a choice whether or not to put up with people who were not good for her and ask for help if she needed it.

Her pier friendship group certainly did not tolerate such behaviour from the other girl. Even though unable to escape her situation on her own accord because of her birth personality and because she did not have the maturity of social coping mechanisms, It was in fact the responsibility of her parents to see that she got the help and support she so desperately needed.

Persons who are emotionally mature enough would hopefully respond to this with reflection and accountability.

How we parent has a huge impact on society in the future. We as parents are responsible for this as our childhood experiences form our adult life. A child is a blank canvas of possibilities, a loving, self-expressing, curious human who wants to connect and wants to share themselves. They are at their core.

At some point, and it happens to all of us, we end up internalising a message that the world gives us that perhaps something is wrong with us and that in order to fit in or survive, or be accepted, or the praise that we are seeking, we have to be somebody other than who we are.

This is where the mind goes sideways and starts to actively tell ourselves that we have got to be like that person or have got to be like this; something is wrong with us if a parent or society is always criticising the way that we look or that we are different in some way from such and such. For example, I'm the only black child in the class, or my family immigrated here.

They can start to see all the places that they are not a part of. All of these thoughts compound and it gets trapped in our mind as we grow up, whereby we can continuously berate and beat ourselves up because of it. We pick apart the things that are wrong and we are relentlessly just focused on what we are not doing.

Of course, we can't eradicate all of this, but as children, if our parents are actively present and most importantly, they are 'present of mind' and can see these things taking shape, then they can take positive actions to support their child through it. A child has a good chance of becoming a happy, stable, confident human being full of self-worth, confidence and self-love with this kind of support.

I know I am an idealist, someone who cherishes and pursues high and noble principles, a visionary in love with their work, but of course, I also understand the practical and impractical considerations. I have this gift and cannot help but see so clearly the consequences of people's unhealthy actions and how they might manifest in the future if and not detected and addressed early on.

I guess it is my gift to want to save people, especially children from unnecessary suffering and heartache.

Chapter 6

Around springtime, something truly miraculous happened. I got back in touch with a cousin who lived in Canada, mainly to gain information on patterns of family behaviour for the content of this book. She, like me, had become a life coach and healer as she was also on a journey to understand and process toxic family practices.

While studying other people's parenting styles and also having unpicked my own family's dysfunctional behaviour patterns, I wanted to see if my experiences with my parents and the effects they had on me in childhood through into adulthood, had been repeated in extended family dynamics and whether she experienced similar patterns of behaviour.

Breaking generational curses takes a lot of hard work and to end those toxic patterns that haunt our families. We all needed to break from the negative expectations assigned to us. I needed to address past trauma. I felt it was imperative to understand how it came to be there and felt it was necessary that this happened. There had been too much trauma repeatedly going on in our family and it was moving into the next generation of our younger family members.

I needed to now have those honest conversations. This cousin had estranged herself from her family for well over ten years because of toxic relationships and struggled to be understood by her parents and one sister in particular.

I knew that she had suffered an eating disorder due to the consequences of this for many years and suffered mental health issues too. There had been an incident when she was 12 years old while staying at a friend's house of her parents. The dad/ husband had touched her in a way that had made her feel uncomfortable but when she years later mentioned the incident to her parents, they dismissed it.

Her parents keeping up appearances with their friends was more important than protecting their daughter and they continued to be friends with these people for over thirty years. My cousin deserved protection and support and this was just one example of many situations with her parents where her feelings were minimised and dismissed, causing her emotional invalidation. Despite her constant efforts to change their minds over the years to no effect, her relationship with her parents had naturally become strained.

Some of the background of this I knew from her sister, my younger cousin who now lived in the UK and was very close to me, almost a sister figure in fact. Our mothers had been estranged for all their lives, but as cousins, we had kept contact in adulthood. Over the years, we were trying to understand what went so terribly wrong with our mothers' relationship as well as my eldest cousin's relationship with her parents.

My mission was to try to understand and break those generational curses, habits and behaviour patterns that had been passed down our family line. Those skills that we had been taught were not necessarily blessed with guidance and amazing lessons; in fact, some of those lessons were very harmful.

My parents, of course, had strived to make sure that the life they led would help us children live a better one, but children practice what they have learnt on their own and from what they have gathered from the generations before them. In some families, this is, however, not automatically a terrible thing; however, how that aligns with where we are at in our own lives can have a negative effect.

Generational curses are passed down through actions of our parents and our own experiences. They are also passed down through storytelling.

We can all remember the stories we were told growing up and the explanations we were given. Some will remember the way in which we were treated. Those are all lessons we take with us into our adult lives. Some of those practices and stories are not necessarily the best to take with us, so what do we do when we are not taught anything better? Growing up, I can remember being taught that the world was a dangerous place and consequently, I became fearful of it.

As a family, we were made to feel that somehow we were unique and special, and that other people were inferior to us, therefore the message I was given growing up was that they were constantly referred to as the plebs, hoi polli, joe bloggs and the great unwashed, negative and damaging views of other people who were less than us. This segmented and isolated us away from humanity.

These stories had some powerful messages and taught me a lot about the outside world and the way I made my way through it. These types of harmful messages keep us connected to our past by causing us to act in a certain way.

Our actions, especially if they are repeated actions, can create roots that become embedded even deeper than the original story.

Dysfunctional behaviour is not always intentional but because of the way my parents were, I had grown up being frightened of the world and the people in it and had kept myself small and isolated. I had little or no interactive skills and was clumsy and awkward in relating to others. My shyness at that time also did not help as it affected my choices of partners.

I accepted whoever had come into my life because, at the time, I really didn't know that many people and without any real discernment, I formed relationships based on neediness and loneliness. The consequences of that had formed my past history. My parents' mindset, I was later to discover, derived from feelings of insecurities and lack of self-esteem, causing psychological projections.

I was not blaming my parents but I did need to understand why they had behaved the way they had. Psychological Projection is a common behaviour phenomenon in which a person projects their own character traits or emotions onto others. It is a form of defence in which unwanted feelings are displaced onto another person, where they then appear as a threat from the external world.

Projection is thought to be an unconscious process that protects the ego from unacceptable thoughts and impulses. By unconsciously taking unwanted emotions or traits you don't like about yourself and attributing them to someone else is projection. A common form of projection occurs when an individual, threatened by their own angry feelings, accuses another of harbouring hostile thoughts and may be a sign of a personality disorder.

Connected to low self-esteem, it is said to be associated with health problems such as depression, anxiety, eating disorders, social phobia, and more importantly, substance abuse and problems in romantic relationships.

Common signs of psychological projection include unprovoked or exaggerated statements about other people, which was very evident to me in my parents growing up. They were very judgemental and critical of others. People who project may claim to know what someone else is thinking or feeling, or they may accuse them of poor behaviour. My eldest cousin in Canada had said that her mother, my aunt, had been a narcissist, and projection and narcissism are connected.

So therefore, we were able to discover that we had a pattern of low self-esteem and narcissism in our family. The worrying thing was that psychological projection often gets observed in those with mental health disorders; it is where the sufferer thinks of themselves first in any given interaction. Projection is not an illness but is a sign of a personality disorder.

Projection does what all defence mechanisms are meant to do, which is to keep discomfort about ourselves at bay and outside of our awareness. People who are most prone to this are those who don't know much about themselves very well, even if they think they do. People who feel inferior and have low self-esteem can fall into this habit of projecting their own feelings onto others.

On the other hand, people who accept their failures and weaknesses, and who are comfortable reflecting on the good, bad and ugly within themselves tend not to project. Projection can look different for each person. Soul searching and reflection, in other words viewing ourselves within with detachment and curiosity, helps to stop projection especially if it's without judgment.

It is human nature, of course, to want to protect yourself from painful or negative feelings and experiences.

Carl Jung, however, stressed that projection is both an inevitable and necessary component in our psychological development as it is one of the primary means by which we can gain an awareness of elements residing in our unconscious. After projecting an element of our unconscious, the healthy thing to do is to recognise the subjective origin of the projection, to withdraw it from the external world, and to integrate this element of our personality into conscious awareness.

This is how we take corrective measures. It can be a difficult task but is crucial in the battle of life, as failure to confront one's shadow side leaves these elements free to grow in scope and influence.

Around the time of my research and discovery, I had been contacted by my youngest cousin's husband in the UK asking for my support as his family was on the cusp of having a major family fallout themselves due to my younger cousin's inherited parenting style. The synchronicity of it could not have come at a better time and was more than a coincidence. It had all of a sudden come to a head at the exact time of my research for this book with my cousin in Canada.

Their 3 teenage children were attacking their mother, stating the damaging effects of her parenting and the abuse they had all felt being on the receiving end of it. The timing was extraordinary, which just goes again to show that there is no such thing as a coincidence. I was able to impart the knowledge I had gained from the cousin in Canada on our families' generational behaviour patterns to my cousin's husband and advised family therapy for them going forward.

A very delicate subject that had to be navigated carefully so that my cousin in the UK did not feel targeted or victimised, but we did not want history repeating itself and we needed to put an end to this destructive negative behaviour. By working together with healthy boundaries and communication skills, in the union of love, trust and compassion, healing can take place and hopefully, estrangement can be avoided.

The wealth of knowledge I have gained from my writing and the work I have done on my healing journey, including all of my greatest transformations that have occurred out of the willingness to endure the quiet storm that always comes before a transformation, has led and prompted me to say that finally, I am in a position to release my parents from the feeling that they have somehow failed with me.

To forgive them for what they had programmed in me in childhood because now I understand the psychology behind it, I can address it. I also release my children from the need to make me proud, so that they can write their own ways, according to their own hearts. I also release my husbands from the past for the obligation to make me feel complete as I now know that I lack nothing in myself.

I have learnt with the help of all the beings that surround me through all time. I thank my grandparents and ancestors with a full heart who met so that today I breathe life. I release them from the faults of the past and from the wishes they did not fulfil, always aware that they did the best they could to resolve their situations within the consciousness that they had at that moment in time. I honour, respect and love them, and recognise their innocence.

I bare my soul before all of their eyes and that is why I hope they know that I do not hide or owe anything other than being faithful to myself and my own existence within the wisdom of my heart.

I am aware that I am fulfilling my life's project, free of visible and invisible family loyalties that may disturb my peace and my happiness, which are my greatest responsibilities. I renounce the role of saviour, the one who always needed to fix everything, of being the one who unites or who fulfils the expectations of others.

With all the learning that I have done and through the *love* I have for myself, I now truly bless my essence and my way of expressing myself. Although, there may be others who may not or cannot understand me. I understand myself now because only I have lived and experienced my story and because now, I know who I am, what I feel what I do, and why I do it.

Because I am a woman of great integrity who has lived and learnt and no longer accepts shame to define her life and who she is. I know my place in this universal puzzle that is life.

As we heal, we become fulfilled. We live lives of meaning and kindness. With compassion for ourselves and others with a purpose that is my life. Because purpose is all about who to be of service to in the world. The writing of this book and creating my own humanity is a testament to my soul and to the person I am today. In all the moments that we choose a new behaviour, we are flooded with both possibilities and grief.

The joy of what we can now create, and the grief for recognising that maybe we waited this long to choose it. When we let go of old ways of being, we become new beings. When we say goodbye to old behaviours, we are creating not only a new self but also the new life that comes along with being that new person.

In early May 2023, I found myself attending a psychic medium fair at the Arthur Findlay College near Stansted Airport in Essex. My eldest daughter invited me and her sister there to experience their facilities. Offering unequalled facilities anywhere in the world in the spiritualist movement, it was a residential centre where students could study spiritualist philosophy and religious practice.

The college offered spiritualist healing and awareness, spiritual and psychic unfolding and kindred disciplines. In 1964, it was gifted to the Spiritualist National Union by J. Arthur Findlay MBE, JP, a former honorary president of the union, and in accordance to his wishes, donated his estate and family home for the advancement of psychic science.

We spent a full day there attending lectures and exploring the college and all it had to offer. We found ourselves in 'the sanctuary', a church-like building with a spiritualist church service going on and hearing psychic mediums bring forth messages from the spirit world through to their loved ones in the congregation. It was both fascinating and interesting.

The college had a museum full of books, apports, automatic scripts, automatic and direct sketches and paintings, paraffin moulds, photographs and other psychic objects. These artefacts took us on a journey to discover how the invisible had been portrayed from Victorian times through to the present day. Intriguing displays of spiritual belief, scientific theories, artistic endeavours, and psychical investigations, it certainly prompted contemplation of the unseen and the world beyond.

By focusing on what we cannot normally see, such as energies, auras, souls, visions, and spirits, it evokes a feeling of awe and wonder. We saw ectoplasmic apparitions in spirit photography, mediumistic and psychic drawings and heard a recording of the famous but controversial Victorian Scottish medium, Helen Duncan, as she channelled spirit through the production of ectoplasm.

On arrival, I had booked a psychic reading with a lovely lady called Jan and I hoped my brother, Andrew, would come through for me. As I proceeded up the grand carpeted staircase to the room where I was to meet her, I took in the grandeur of the college. Grade 11 listed, Stansted Hall was originally the country seat of the Earls of Essex during the reign of Henry VIII of England and had been utilised by man for at least 2,000 years.

Some years ago, a Roman villa was discovered on land nearby and was part of a Roman settlement. Since the 14th century, there have been various halls built on the site but sadly, there have been many fires which destroyed the buildings over the years. Now built of decorative Bath stone in the Jacobean style with Victorian building techniques in 1871, the building had reclaimed 16th century wood panelling throughout and magnificent Adam fireplaces.

The ceilings were decorated in ornate plaster mouldings which added to its impressive grandeur. The grounds and landscaping of Stansted Hall Estate date back to the 12th century, where a park was mentioned in the Domesday book of 1066. Today, it is home to some 776 trees, which are heritage trees planted in 1770. It is a beautiful and historic place.

Arriving at the designated room for my reading, I was greeted by Jan. As I sat down, she immediately told me that my system was overloaded and that I needed to learn how to manage my energy while exploring my spiritual and psychotherapy work. I was also told not to force the future ahead of me but to allow it to unfold gently. Also, I was not to force my belief system on those who were not ready to receive it as it could be damaging to them.

She gave me an analogy of a person going into a restaurant and being served every single meal on the menu telling me that they could not possibly digest everything in front of them. I was then asked what I hoped to get from the session. I told her I wanted to connect with my brother. She instantly told me that he was skipping around with glee and happiness and wanted me to know that he was very excited about the work I was doing and that we would work together.

He would be helping me achieve this from the spirit world. She encouraged me to take one of her courses at the college where her specialist field of work was art mediumship. She said that my brother could communicate through that but I knew Andrew could communicate in other ways and anyway, I was useless at art and drawing.

I asked her if she could tell me anything of his passing. All she said was that he did not like it here and wanted to leave. It was a short 20-minute session because there were others coming after me for their own readings. I left knowing the path I was on with my books was a necessary path to share with those who were ready to hear it.

Afterwards, I caught up with my girls who had their own readings elsewhere in the building. I heard that both their grandfathers had been present in spirit. We then went for an energy healing session. It had all been an interesting visit but I had this strong sensation after we left of not wanting any more contact with the dead. I felt the time had come for me to live my life fully and completely. I now knew that anytime I wanted to speak to my deceased loved ones, I had a phone.

Chapter 7

At the end of May 2023, I turned 60 years old. My family and friends threw a fabulous birthday party for me at a hotel in Tunbridge Wells. Finally, I had achieved what I had set out to do in the writing of my memoirs, which was to have love, peace and harmony with those who had been involved in my life despite all of our differences.

I now understand that acceptance is the ability to see that others have a right to be their own unique person, which means having a right to their own thoughts, feelings and opinions. When we accept people for who they are, we let go of our desire to change them. We let them feel the way they want to feel, we let them be different and think differently from us.

Everyone is different in one way or another. Once we understand this truth, we can stop trying to change them into the people we want them to be and start accepting them for who they are. Acceptance of others' 'feelings' is not easy when people act differently than we do. We all have trouble accepting those who are different. By learning the skill of empathy, we will be better able to understand ourselves and those who are different from us.

With feelings, there is no right or wrong answer. So instead of trying to control or change other people's feelings, we must allow them to have feelings without telling them how they should feel. Empathetic people understand that feelings are difficult to control and they accept others' feelings for what they are.

How boring life would be if we were all the same. If everyone looked the same, had the same experiences, the same interests, and the same personality; we would surely lose interest in each other very quickly. Luckily, each of us has a unique set of qualities and characteristics that make us different. Even though we know that these differences are for the best, sometimes we feel uncomfortable with these differences. It is natural, in this case, to try to change people, or avoid them.

Being empathic means having an open mind and accepting these unique differences. The next time we are around someone who appears to be our polar opposite, let's challenge ourselves to get to know them better. If we find out more about a person, maybe we will have something in common and actually not be so different as perhaps we first thought.

Only through this exercise can we truly become discerning and inquisitive and decide whether it is safe or not to let that person into our lives. I have learnt not to be quick to judge as it's so easy to look at another person and point out their flaws. Sometimes we judge and criticise without realising it. The more challenging and empathetic response would be to point out the good in each person.

When we accept others as they are, it means we understand that they are doing the best that they can do at the time. I'm sure if they could do better they would.

By comparing we only make ourselves unhappy as there is always going to be someone who is better, smarter or richer. Instead, we must accept that each person is on a different path in life. Acceptance will make us become a more positive and happier person. With this in mind, I go forth in what I guess to be the best possible years left of my life. I now focus on enjoying the rest of my life, fully knowing that in wisdom, I have the best possible tools to live my very best life.

THE END